the

Healing Light

of

Angels

About the Author

Raven Keyes (New York) is a Reiki master, teacher, certified hypnotherapist, and guided meditation instructor. She was part of the original Complementary Alternative Medicine program at Columbia Presbyterian Hospital led by Dr. Mehmet Oz. In the world of professional sports, Raven has brought Reiki to athletes in the NFL and the NBA. Featured in national magazines such as *Vogue* and *W*, she was named "Best Reiki Master in New York" by *New York Magazine* and is a regular contributor to *Reiki News* and a previous contributor to *Psychology Today*.

Transforming Your Past, Present & Future
with Divine Energy

the

Healing Light

of

Angels

RAVEN KEYES

Llewellyn Publications
Woodbury, Minnesota

First Edition
First Printing, 2015

Cover art: iStockphoto.com/15000955/©Jeja
        iStockphoto.com/20691827/©Antagain
Cover design by Ellen Lawson
Editing by Stephanie Finne

Llewellyn Publications is a registered trademark of Llewellyn Worldwide, Ltd.

Library of Congress Cataloging-in-Publication Data (Pending)
ISBN: 978-0-7387-4154-3

Llewellyn Worldwide Ltd. does not participate in, endorse, or have any authority or responsibility concerning private business transactions between our authors and the public.

All mail addressed to the author is forwarded but the publisher cannot, unless specifically instructed by the author, give out an address or phone number.

Any Internet references contained in this work are current at publication time, but the publisher cannot guarantee that a specific location will continue to be maintained. Please refer to the publisher's website for links to authors' websites and other sources.

Llewellyn Publications
A Division of Llewellyn Worldwide, Ltd.
2143 Wooddale Drive
Woodbury, MN 55125-2989, U.S.A.
www.llewellyn.com

Printed in the United States of America

Other books by Raven Keyes

The Healing Power of Reiki

Dedicated to the Archangel Gabriel,
With all my love

Contents

CHAPTER 9:
Angels Healing the Healer / 171

Acknowledgments

I give thanks to the divine spirits of Avalon for welcoming me into wondrous beauty and supporting me as I wrote a major portion of this book. No words can express my gratitude to Mascha and Karyn Boniface, who provided a safe haven for me as I wrote in England and took me to magical places around Glastonbury that I never knew existed. I thank Gwynn Ap Nudd for leading me through portals to see for myself the deeply divine aspects of our most sacred Earth. And, of course, I give my heartfelt thanks to Archangel Gabriel and to all the other angels who sat with me as I wrote the words that turned into chapters, all graced with their love.

Thanks also to my family; my agent, Brandi Bowles; my editor, Angela Wix; and to all those at Llewellyn Worldwide who looked after every aspect of my book with such care.

The good physician treats the disease;
the great physician treats the patient
who has the disease.

—WILLIAM OSLER

By Dr. Ketan K. Badani, MD

I was raised in an environment of alternative and Ayurvedic medicine. My parents and relatives always had a "remedy" for all ailments, a remedy that did not involve pills or other traditional therapy. That is not to say that I have practiced medicine that way; I am very much an allopathic doctor. I am a minimally invasive robotic surgeon, so if a patient has prostate or kidney cancer, I remove it. If there is a mechanical problem with the kidney, I will fix it. I have a busy practice, and I constantly and consciously endeavor to help all my patients. However, most surgeons' approach to curing a disease is very mechanical in nature. Now, I am not saying we are not innovative; I have dedicated my research to surgical technology innovation and helping improve the outcome for patients requiring prostate or kidney surgery using minimally invasive approaches. However, there is more to curing a disease than treating the physical problem; I now truly believe it.

My parents are immigrants from India, and they were raised in a culture and time that did not endorse Western medicine as the only or even the primary recourse. As such, I was exposed early in life to alternative and complementary medicine. Certainly, these practices were mostly empirical in nature, with not a lot of facts, literature, or even any science behind them; we just believed that they worked. Perhaps that is why when I went to medical school I dove into the "real science" and needed facts to support any medical treatments; due to this shift in thinking, I went further toward traditional Western medicine and basically dismissed anything else.

That all changed when I met Raven Keyes. She came to my office with a kidney problem, and she needed surgery. She will detail the story later in this book. However, this encounter was meaningful for me in many important ways. She brought a trusted friend with her, a Reiki master, and requested that her friend be present during the surgery in the operating room to perform Reiki on her. DURING THE SURGERY! Now, I have seen many things in my years of surgical practice, but this was a first. I could not imagine why she would want a friend in the OR during her operation, which has to be one of the most personal and private events that is almost never open to friends and family. I am not a closed-minded person. I am traditional in many ways but open to new ideas. I did not dismiss her request, crazy as it sounded to me at the time. If Raven felt this would help her heal, who was I to think otherwise, so long as there was no obvious and clear danger? This definitely got me to think about the patient as a whole, not just a single problem. If she truly believed that Reiki would assist her during surgery, then maybe her mental calmness alone would be helpful to her healing, and that was reason enough for me.

Raven's Reiki master came to her surgery and did her work unobtrusively and without coming in the way of the surgical team throughout the entire operation. Raven's particular procedure was very difficult, to say the least, due partially to years of infection and scarring of her kidney. In the end, all went well. Raven had one of the fastest and smoothest recoveries from a surgery like this that I have ever seen. She went home the day after her surgery, but more than that, when I saw her one week later in my office, she was almost back to normal. All the feeling of sickness and ill health she had prior to surgery was completely gone, and she was refreshed and new again. Remarkable. When I told Raven how pleased I was with the results, she surprised me yet again by telling me she felt her accelerated healing was orchestrated by angels. What a shock! But her statement caused me to further consider the possible connection between body and mind, and how a spiritual belief might have a positive effect on outcome.

I had my first Reiki session with Raven a short time afterward. She had invited me during her postoperative visit. I was curious at this point; was there more to this than I knew and understood? At the very least, I reasoned, it would be a relaxing experience after a long day in the operating room. So why not? Well, I went to Raven's office for my session. Raven greeted me warmly, and immediately I felt calm and welcome. As I lay on her table, I thought I would probably fall asleep and get a good nap out of the whole thing. I could not have been more wrong. Instantly, I could feel an intense heat emanating from her hands; everywhere she went, without even touching me, I could feel where her hands were. I couldn't believe it. I thought she was using a heater or steam, and I would open my eyes every so often to check, but it was just her hands transmitting energy. In our discussion after it was over, Raven told me that angels had been helping her to deliver the Reiki. I can't speak to her experience—all I can say is that the session was incredible for me.

Just writing these words makes me realize how far I have come in understanding and appreciating Reiki as a form of healing. The session lasted for over one hour, and the experience was like nothing that I could have imagined. I not only felt refreshed and calm, but I also experienced the sensation of receiving energy and strength that I would not have imagined in my allopathic world.

I now offer Reiki, as well as other complementary treatments, to all my patients undergoing surgery. I have learned from Raven that disease is not solely the physical ailment, but the entire person: physical, mental, and spiritual. Learning should always be lifelong, and I have learned the importance of treating the patient, not just the disease.

—Ketan K. Badani, MD

Vice Chair of Urology and Robotic Operations—
    Mount Sinai Health System

Professor of Urology—Icahn School of Medicine,
    Mount Sinai Hospital

Introduction

My name is Raven Keyes, and I am a Reiki master assisted by the spiritual beings we call angels. Reiki (pronounced *ray-key)* is a healing practice that was formally established in the early 1900s by Dr. Mikao Usui. Through the processes he left behind in his teachings, Reiki masters are trained to bring the healing power of the universe (Reiki) into their hands. They then place their palms in a series of hand positions on or just over a client's body in order to restore balance, bring peace, and stimulate the body's natural ability to heal itself.

For me, when the door to Reiki opened, an angel came through it and took up residence in my heart. Soon after, more angels followed and expanded their workings with me beyond just Reiki. They have led me to spiritual practices out of the mainstream and even introduced me to beings in other realms, such as faeries, power animals, and spirit guides.

A major portion of the work I continue to do is in the world of medicine, where I work alongside surgeons and doctors to bring Reiki to their patients. Yet none of this would have ever happened without the angels.

In my last book, *The Healing Power of Reiki*, I described the many situations in which I've provided Reiki, some of them quite extraordinary. I brought readers to operating rooms, to the locker room of the New York Giants football team, and to Ground Zero in New York City after September 11, 2001. Doctors, patients, professional athletes, and rescue and recovery workers I met after 9/11 were introduced. In this book, a few of the same characters reappear, but this time to show just how big a part the angels played in bringing us together. You will also get to meet many new characters in stories that reveal how angels can help to heal the past, shape the present, and mold the future.

Angels opened within me an awareness of their wondrous love while teaching me about their powers. They assist with many different kinds of issues that require transformation. They have traveled with me across oceans, up mountainsides, and to many other locations where they have helped me with my work. And they do the same for you.

The truth is, no matter who we are or how we have been raised, no matter how much trauma we may have suffered as children or as adults, the angels can help us let go of the past and start a new future that is founded in love and blessings. Whether the effects of our past manifest in big or small ways, the angels can always help us get rid of things we don't need or want and start over.

What Is This Book?

The stories I am about to tell give insight into how my own guardian angel and other angels have administered love to heal me, brought help to those I care for, and provided assistance to me as a Reiki master, meditation teacher, workshop leader, and overall concerned human being. The aid they have provided as I work with people, the spirits of the deceased, land spirits, and other kinds of spiritual beings has been truly remarkable. I hope my stories will inspire others to step out along the road with angels. As encouragement to do so, I share the messages the angels have given to me through the years that were never meant just for me—they are for every one of us who lives on Earth.

This book carries timely messages because there is just so much healing that is needed on our beautiful planet! With illness, war, natural disasters, violent human behavior, and terrorist events that leave people traumatized, it's soothing, and even imperative, for us to know that we can turn to the angels for assistance. This is something worth speaking about, because as our world continues to whirl in ever more confusing and disturbing ways, the angels wish to help us by sharing their knowledge and their loving healing powers with as many people as possible.

Included with the stories are meditations and exercises you can do that will help you in your quest to connect with or strengthen your ties to angels. Repeating the same process of entering meditation is very effective. Traveling the same road makes getting into a meditative state quicker and easier, so I am going to use the technique of repetition here and there.

I recommend strongly that you do the meditations and exercises with a journal and a pen close by so you can record your experiences. The recording of these workings will become a great treasure trove of proof of your ever-unfolding life and your connections to these vast and powerful angelic beings.

How This Book Is Organized

This book offers a bird's-eye view into my life with the angels and all the different ways in which they have helped me through the years—professionally, personally, and when working with other kinds of spirits.

First, we will encounter the angels as I've come to know them, providing a foundation for who and what these spiritual beings are. From there, I'll move on to explain what it took to reconnect with my angel in adulthood and how angels have protected me in different situations. In chapter 4, we'll get into stories of angels assisting me in my work as a professional Reiki master and teacher. I'll continue on to describe my work with the breast cancer patients I've worked with in tandem with a well-known surgeon. But the angels don't only work with us to heal our bodies. I describe the ways in which the angels have assisted me in my world travels through special blessings and in healing the land and places that have experienced trauma. Finally, we'll delve into how angels can heal the effects of past trauma and the ways in which Gabriel and the angels assisted me in my own healing.

Each chapter contains personal stories about specific ways in which the angelic realm has assisted me. Also included are meditations and exercises that bring readers into an ever-deepening connection with the angels. The meditations and exercises can be done as self-practice or in groups. They can be read from the book, recorded ahead of time for listening, or read aloud by a teacher or a friend. Choose the way that works best for you. When doing sacred work, just relax and let things unfold without putting pressure on yourself or deciding beforehand how it is "supposed" to work. The angels will find you in whatever way suits you best, so you might hear them, feel them, sense them, or just know they are there. Most people don't physically see them, but all ways of perceiving the angels are perfect and powerful!

Take what you can use from my experiences and, as with all information that comes your way, disregard whatever doesn't feel right to you. I say "feel" because some of what you read may not fit into the mental constructs of current belief systems or how reality has been described to us by our societies. When it comes to your own interaction with angels, discern what resonates with you *right now*. Things can change in the future, but all that matters is how you feel in this moment, and how you wish to proceed in a way that feels like you are best taking care of yourself.

I hope to inspire others by giving insight into how angels have helped me and my clients with everything under the sun. Toward that end, my prayer as we begin is: *I ask to be an instrument in service to the angels by bringing awareness of their powers into the consciousness of the world to the best of my ability. I ask the angels to imbue the words on these pages with the emotions necessary to feel what it's like to walk with angels as helpers, guardians, and even—where appropriate—as "healing partners."*

Angels have no philosophy but love.

—TERRI GUILLEMETS

CHAPTER 1

Encountering Angels

Before we begin your personal introduction with the angels, I'd like to start by sharing with you just how my connection with the angelic realm began.

One afternoon when I was just a little girl, I had an accident that changed everything. Right after my family had enjoyed lunch, graciously presented to us by my grandmother, I was running out the door of her cozy apartment to what I thought would be just another regular afternoon of playing with the neighborhood kids. Instead, I fell down my grandmother's stairs, hitting my head on the landing at the bottom so hard that I was knocked unconscious. I cried wretchedly as I began to regain consciousness because my head hurt so much. Not only that, I was seeing double.

Everyone felt terrible about my falling. My mom and dad hovered around me while my grandmother held me in her arms. Everyone was trying to figure out whether or not I was seriously hurt.

"I know," said my grandmother, "let's go look at your corn plant! That will make you feel better."

I was carried outside to look at that newly sprouting wonder, which was becoming a pretty green stalk up against the pale stone on the south side of the garage. I did feel a bit cheered looking at it, but I was seeing it with blurred vision, and I had a sharp pain in the front of my head. All I wanted was to lie down and go to sleep.

The next thing I can remember is that I was alone. To this day, I can't explain it. I just remember feeling earth under my head as soft as any pillow and sweet-smelling grasses beneath me that gave me the feeling of "home."

I looked up and saw a beautiful golden being kneeling next to me on the grass. A brilliant light was shining from within him that went beyond his body, encasing him in white gold. He gazed at me with such loving eyes that I felt my heart catch with happiness as I held up my arms to him. He picked me up and gathered me close to his chest in a tender hug. He told me, "Don't worry, child, you are going to be all right." He smiled ever so sweetly as he continued, "I'm always with you, helping you with your life." As he held me in his arms, I felt washed in love. I knew I was safe and that I was being healed. Joy flooded through my heart and I wanted to stay in his arms forever. I didn't know it at the time, but this would be the first of many memorable encounters with an angel in my lifetime.

I recovered quickly from the fall and my childhood continued on happily afterward, full of adventures peopled with my amazing relatives. My grandmother and my great-aunties were very important parts of my upbringing. This powerful force of loving women who carried the old knowledge of our ancestors from Scotland and Poland seemed positively magical to me! They never tired of showing me the beauty and majesty of life and of all the ways in which things were connected to each other.

On summer days, as we relaxed sitting in the grass, Gram would ask me, "What do you feel?" Squinting her hazel eyes, she would run her hands through the sun-drenched clover. Then closing her eyes, she would say, "There's more here than you can see!" Within moments, with her eyes still closed, she would almost always pluck a four-leaf clover out of the mass of green, saying things like, "Look at this. I found us more good luck." Pure and natural magic!

Gram and her kindred taught me about plants, trees, the hidden world behind the one we could see, and the healing properties inherent in all the nature around us. Gram always administered natural remedies to us when we were sick, and she taught me things, such as how to get my skin to stop stinging when I wandered into nettles by accident. She talked to me about the meanings of my dreams and taught me little prayers, including "Angels bless and angels keep, angels guard me while I sleep. Bless my heart and bless my home, bless my spirit as I roam. Guide and guard me through the night and wake me with the morning's light."

Based on the wise guidance of our grandmother and our great-aunties, my sisters and I established all kinds of supernatural connections. We knew things about the creatures in our environment that most people never even thought about. For example, salamanders (with their ability to regrow tails) must certainly hold mystery within them and should be talked to and treated with respect. Based on stories from old books that were read to us, we suspected that the frogs and toads we found in the field next door to where we lived were from fairyland and we treated them with love. The trees that grew around our house all had their own personalities, and we felt a deep connection with them. We learned so much about the flow of life from climbing in their branches, feeling their wisdom through our skin, and listening to the messages blowing through their leaves.

As I look back on my childhood days, I give thanks for those who helped me recognize the significance of what was around me. These intimate interactions and relationships with the things in our immediate environment made me brave and willing to look beyond the obvious, through the veil to the magical, the mysterious, and the sacred.

All these good things worked together to create the experiences I started having nearly every night from about the age of seven. The children in my family were not raised in the structure of any particular religious dogma. For us, nature was the face of God. But we weren't kept in the dark about belief systems either. Somewhere along the way, my mom (who had been raised Catholic) told me that the Blessed Mother Mary had been visited by the Archangel Gabriel, who informed her that she would give birth to Jesus. This was simply amazing news to me and inspired me to start a nightly game called "talking to angels." Once everyone else was asleep, I would whisper those little prayers taught to me by Gram, and then sparkles would fill my room. When sleep came to find me, it would take me sweetly into its bliss while I was enthralled in the midst of heartwarming conversations with divine beings, including the one who had come after my fall.

Adolescent Disconnect

In all the emotion and drama of growing into my teenage years, I forgot all about the angels along with every one of my spiritual connections to nature. I repeat: *I forgot all about them*—just when I needed them the most! I often wonder how many others have had the same experience.

As children, we are taught to dream. We are exposed to mermaids and faeries, introduced to Peter Pan and the Lost Boys, told stories of other realms that can be glimpsed through a veil, and generally ushered into the magical by what our culture creates for children. The problem is, most of the adults around us aren't really serious about any of this, so when we start to grow up, they expect us to give it all up easily and without any grieving for what has become important to us. Now we must let go of our sight into the spiritual, along with the doorways we have found into other worlds. In my case, I was certainly lucky to have Gram and the magical women who helped raise me.

It's just a fact of life that it was my fate to grow up where and when I did. I was expected to enter high school at age fourteen, leaving behind all the wild magic I had come to love. I was told that it was now time to grow up and "stop with the make-believe." I would now be entering a huge new school filled with thousands of students, and I was expected to make my way bravely on my own. My parents lovingly and confidently sent me out into what was, for me, a scary new world populated by strangers. I was terrified!

The loss I felt for my childhood days and for the connections I had to angels and magical beings was overwhelming. Faith in myself came to an abrupt end, along with faith in everything else I thought I knew. The angels dissolved into the mists of my own past, relegated to that group of "made-up" childhood things, like Santa Claus and the tooth fairy.

It wasn't until I was an adult that the doors to my spiritual life began to reopen. A door began to creak open sometime later with the pronouncement of my then three-year-old son that he had come to me from another life in which he had died in an accident, and then again with the appearance of my spirit guide, Little Raven. It opened further still when I began my Reiki training. That's when the angel I had known in childhood came back into my awareness. Of course, by the time this happened, I had learned to invest my faith in "the real world," which was seriously problematic when it came to believing in anything outside the ordinary. But with the patience of the angels and their continued presentation of proof, I returned to my true self—and to them—once more.

I hope that by sharing my story, you'll see that it's okay to not believe until you receive your own proof. By working through the practices I provide in each chapter, you'll work your way to finding, or strengthening, your belief.

Angels Predate Religion

Connections with angels have been recorded throughout history. Long before our current religions came into being, our ancestors already had a name for them. The earliest form of the word "angel" appears in the language of the Mycenaeans, a people who flourished at the end of the Bronze Age of ancient Greece between 1600 BC and 1100 BC. Back in those times, the word for "angel" indicated a supernatural being or spirit from beyond the everyday realm of humankind. In the beginning of their mention, they were not connected to one particular god.

Since angels predate any religious mention of them, they are not religious beings. In the past, the beings we call *angels* were certainly known to our ancestors, although they might have been called something very different. The more I've immersed myself in the study of ancient spiritual thought and practices, the more I've come to understand the innate ability, and even the need, we humans have always had to connect to the greater powers both seen and unseen that are all around us. For we humans, at least, it becomes necessary to categorize these energies in order to work with them, so we give them names.

As time went by and religions developed, angels were mentioned in Hebrew and in Latin. Eventually, a melding of the Old English/Germanic *engel* and the Old French *angele* resulted in the word "angel." Only two angels are mentioned in the Bible by name. The name Gabriel appears four times—twice when he arrives to interpret the visions of Daniel (Daniel 8–9), once when he announced the birth of John the Baptist to John's father (Luke 1:11–20), and a final time during the famous visitation with Mary to tell her she would give birth to Jesus (Luke 1:26–38). Michael is mentioned several times in the books of Daniel, Jude, and Revelations. It is noted in Psalm 68:17, Revelation 5:11, and Isaiah 40:26 that there are "innumerable angels" and that God knows all their names.

Michael and Gabriel along with Ariel (Uriel) and Raphael, are all mentioned in the book of Enoch (20:1–8). There it is said that Michael is set over the best parts of mankind, Gabriel is set over Paradise, Ariel is set over the world, and Raphael is set over the spirits of men.

Further traditional writings about Ariel appear in Apocrypha as well as in Jewish and Christian mysticism. Ariel appears in the Hebrew Bible as an archangel whose name means "Lion of God." It is said that Ariel guards us as we walk the spiritual path. This fits in with some of the Gnostic texts that describe Ariel as a "controller of demons." It is also said that Ariel assists Raphael in the healing arts.

In Judaism and Christianity, Raphael is an archangel who performs every kind of healing. Raphael is associated with stirring the water at the healing pool of Bethesda in the Gospel of John and is the guardian of pilgrims on their journeys. There is a story in the book of Tobit (Tobias) of Raphael healing Tobias's eyes with the gallbladder of a fish.

In the three religions of Judaism, Christianity, and Islam, angels came to be described as "messengers of God." But what about the times before these religions, when people knew many gods—and goddesses even? My heart tells me there were still angels in the mix, because angels have always been a part of the universe's life.

What Are Angels?

What are angels really? And why do they matter? Over time, I've come to realize that angels are more than we can comprehend mentally. They can only be understood with and through the heart. The angels lead all of us into our own infinite possibilities to affect positive change in our own lives and in the world.

I know that in most theology, angels are thought to be holier than us and very separate from every other being except God. Yet, the angels themselves have taught me that although we may be different from each other, we are not separate. All those who wish to participate in accomplishing the goals of transformation, healing, joy, and peace are invited to assist, whether angel, human, or other kind of being.

Angels can be described as a wondrous energy field of pure, divine love that presents to us in response to our unique needs. This is why angels may show up in different ways to different people. It all depends on who is calling upon them, what their needs are at the moment, and their easiest way to perceive. Some people see, hear, sense, feel, or just know. There's no best or better; there's just how each one of us is wired for spiritual connection.

Any communication with one angel is really a communication with the whole energy band of pure love they inhabit. In other words, one angel brings knowledge from, and speaks for, the entire realm.

Angels reveal themselves in whatever way will make it possible for their messages to be received. For example, while one person perceives a particular angel in a certain way, the next person might experience the very same angel in a completely *different* way. Likewise, depending on the person calling on them, the light the angel emanates might be experienced as golden, white, pink, or even blue. There is no "correct" or "incorrect" way in which to perceive them—it's all about how each one of us operates individually.

There have been times when my awareness has opened up and I have experienced the totality of the profound love the angels carry. When those times have come, they have been fleeting, because (quite frankly) the power of that kind of joy is overwhelming. It would be counterproductive to have an experience like that while driving a car or shopping for groceries in the supermarket! Yet that state of divine connection fosters one of the strongest times in which to make a request of the angels—and that's exactly what it is, a request for help, not a prayer. Yet angels sometimes appear after prayer. The prayers that bring angels often come in times of great personal trial.

No matter who we are, we have help available to us—help that brings awareness and the peace of inner balance. All we ever have to do is ask. Living life in partnership with angels is really uplifting. To those who have a healing practice, I lovingly suggest that you "take up" with your own angel if you haven't done so already; there's nothing more heartwarming or effective! It's also comforting to know that everything is not resting on your shoulders alone.

How I Work with the Archangels

Traditionally, Archangel Michael's name means "he who is like God." Michael can protect us physically and energetically when we ask for his help. He removes fears and encourages confidence.

Archangel Gabriel's name means "God is my strength." He is considered to be a messenger. He assists with communication and writing projects and also helps parents with their children. Also, Gabriel is oftentimes called upon for aid when a couple is having difficulty conceiving a child.

Archangel Ariel's name means "Light of God." He is said to bring intelligence, inspiration, and illumination.

Archangel Raphael's name means "God heals." Sometimes referred to as "heaven's physician," Raphael is said to bring physical healing as well as guardianship to travelers.

I have my own unique relationship with the four archangels, which may or may not match up to anything you have ever heard about them. In the exploration of angels, everyone finds their own way of knowing and working with them. For me, it has been a natural progression to communicate the most with Gabriel and to ask for special help from Michael. I consult much less frequently with Ariel and Raphael.

The way in which Ariel and Raphael have presented themselves to me is by holding me in a vertical channel of energy, with Ariel a vast presence above me and Raphael's enormous power extending below me. In my way of working with them, Ariel holds the knowledge of eternity and is the angel I consult if I want to gain clarity about something in the past or insight for the future. Raphael holds the energy of freedom, so if I need advice about how to create breathing room for growth in any situation, I ask to connect with Raphael.

The workings I do with Ariel and Raphael are usually done in meditation. Whenever I ask to connect with them, I feel myself held in that vertical axis of power, and I experience my essence (spirit) as "free forever." In any ceremonies or rituals I perform, I call Ariel in when I honor the north energies and Raphael for the south. For me, they are the archangels of "bestowing."

Gabriel is with me all the time as I go through my life—he's just there, walking behind me or at my side. Michael comes to me immediately whenever I call to him. Michael does clearing work for me and for my clients. In ceremony, Gabriel is of the east, and Michael is of the west. In my workings, they are the archangels of "action."

But no matter how we perceive the archangels, and no matter how we work with them, they always hold the loving power that can heal and transform anything they touch.

Angels in Modern Medicine

Because a major portion of my work is in assisting patients of doctors who support integrative medicine, there are several stories included here regarding Reiki clients and how angels have helped them during sessions. Clinical proof is mounting that shows how receiving Reiki while undergoing standard medical treatment brings a better experience for the patient. Reiki can even effect positive physical changes. All of this special work enhances the efforts and goals of the doctors I work with. As the patient wends their way back to health, the more buoyant emotional, mental, and spiritual states inspired by angel-infused Reiki are of vast usefulness to them in their healing process.

Whether they were sent by a friend or a doctor, or even found me on the Internet, many of my clients are facing allopathic medical treatments that are severe and often terrifying. Helping them find the courage to endure the prescribed remedies is usually one of the first challenges we face, and this is where the angels "come to save the day," literally. I can't begin to tell you how many times I've relied on angelic inspiration while talking to my clients about their allopathic treatments.

As a professional Reiki master, I go into surgery as well as train others for important medical work. Because I connect with the angelic realm as part of my Reiki practice, angels are right there in the operating room, lending me their aid by providing extra protection and supplying divine love to the patient, as well as to the doctors and technicians!

It's true there are many Reiki teachers and practitioners who do not work with angels, but with the seriousness of the work I do, I wouldn't have it any other way. Every Reiki master I teach meets their guardian angel as part of their training, and most of those I've trained choose to work with angelic support.

Communicating with Angels

The ways in which I've been able to communicate with Gabriel and the angels have developed and strengthened over the years as I've slowly learned to trust myself. In my current communications, meanings are impressed into my emotional body while I hear Gabriel's words. That is to say, my emotions let me know the tone and truth of what I am hearing. For example, recently one of my breast cancer clients came to my office for an emergency Reiki session because she was experiencing an attack of hysteria. As I held her hand while she cried, I experienced the feeling of "certainty beyond doubt" as Gabriel said, "Her symptoms are withdrawal from the medication she was taking." I know absolutely nothing about the medicines oncologists prescribe for their patients. I simply told her what Gabriel had said and suggested she ask her doctor. With the assistance of Gabriel and her guardian angel, the Reiki session calmed her, and when she saw her oncologist a few days later, Gabriel's words were confirmed. A state of withdrawal had been brought on by the change in her medication, which had upset her hormonal balance, causing hysteria.

Being able to "feel" the messages is certainly wondrous, yet all of my communication with angels began with the first step of automatic writing.

Automatic Writing with Angels

Automatic writing is a powerful way to launch your communication with angels. It really is a wonderful and encouraging experience—a fantastic way to get your own information.

There are two main ways I do automatic writing, both of which I will describe below. However, before we begin, let your intention be that you will be gentle with yourself and that you will experiment by allowing simple trust in what comes through. Then all you have to do is wait to see what happens. Keep in mind that in the beginning, almost everyone has the feeling of "I made it up." Accept that as a common reaction, and don't just automatically reject the information you get. Be willing to pay attention to the things that begin to happen around you that bring confirmation of what you receive in the transmissions, and let yourself notice how you are shaped by the messages themselves. Keep in mind that this is you giving yourself permission to trust in your own inner way of knowing, which will crack open the door through which your guardian angel will be able to step through to reach you.

So just stop for a moment, close your eyes, and say, "thank you." *Thank you* is a powerful tool that automatically raises your vibrations. The more you can be in a state of thanks, the faster things can happen. Even if you have a lot of troubles right now, you can at least say "thank you" to the air you are breathing for keeping you alive, to the water in your glass for the hydration it brings to your body, to the earth under your feet for giving you a place to be, and to the angels in advance for what is going to come to you.

What Is Automatic Writing?

I want to explain to anyone who might not be familiar with it how automatic writing happens for me so you can use it as a guide. As a first step, I quiet myself to enter a state of inner calm and prayer. Next, I write a question or a comment in my journal and simply wait for the response. Sometimes I hear the response, and sometimes I just write it down as if I'm taking dictation. The only limitation on what gets written down comes from me. As I start to hear the words, they sometimes come so quickly that I can't write them down fast enough and some of the information does not make it to the page. The feelings that are part of the experiences are so beautiful and strong that there just *aren't* any words to convey them.

In the times when I don't hear the words, it's as if I'm taking dictation, only it happens in a different way. In those cases, my handwriting changes from my usual penmanship because my hand moves as the pen is guided across the page. In these cases, I experience the accompanying feelings of what is being written while my hand writes the words.

When I first started to do automatic writing, it happened without any planning on my part. I would be going along, writing in my journal, when suddenly a communication would come through. In the beginning, the information I received was helpful to me personally. Before long, I began to write down things that seemed to be universal in nature. These newer transmissions were accompanied by states of pure ecstasy and incredible love.

Beginning a Practice of Automatic Writing

In my experience, the first way to get comfortable with this procedure is to wake up a little earlier than usual in order to write three freeform pages in your journal. I learned to do this from Julia Cameron's book *The Artist's Way* and have used it often—it works like a charm to initiate communication with angels!

In the beginning, it's best to do as Cameron advises: make a commitment to yourself to write three pages each morning for at least a month. This really gets the energy flowing. You get up and start writing anything that comes to mind without thinking about it. If you feel stuck, you can just write the same thing over and over again until something else comes— for example, "I don't have anything more to say. I don't have anything more to say." By being committed to writing the three pages, before you know it, something else will start to come through, and pretty soon you will start to write down things you never knew anything about. It will just happen naturally! I predict that you will be very surprised at what this brings out of and to you.

Once you are accustomed to doing this, you can try the second way, which is to sit comfortably with your journal and a pen close by when you want to get an answer to a question. Start by simply focusing on your breathing. Notice the air going in and out across the tips of your nostrils, and start to thank the air for keeping you alive. Once you feel relaxed, call golden light to surround you as you pick up your journal and write down the question you'd like to get an answer to. Then move your awareness into your heart center in the middle of your chest and just wait.

Write down anything that begins to come to you, whether it's something you feel, hear, see, or sense—just let it happen, without trying to control or edit the experience. Sometimes in the beginning, things come in a very subtle way, and sometimes when you start to write the transmission down it doesn't seem to be making any sense, but stick with it. You'll be amazed at what will be revealed to you, if you just wait and allow everything to naturally unfold. I predict that you will be very glad you asked, because in my experience, depending on the situation, the information the angels provide can bring healing, surprise, encouragement, and delight, depending on what you need!

This is a good time in which to share a bit of automatic writing that came through in the beginning when I was so afraid and overwhelmed with doubt about what was happening to me. No matter what your current state of mind (or heart) might be, I believe this will be of help to you, too. I received this in a state of overwhelming doubt and fear. I decided to write down a question, and I got an answer. I hope it helps you as much as it helped me.

"Why should I be allowed to receive messages from angels? I am nobody."

Everybody is special. A specialness that is part of the One, which is the most special thing of all in all its many parts. You are no different. … You are a representative of everyone as one of many. All share in the Oneness. All are the One. … Trust yourself. You have decided that only certain attributes are holy. What you fail to realize is the completeness—the light can only be understood as Light because of the darkness. Be gentle with yourself, please.

So remember this as you're working through the exercises and developing your relationship with the angels.

Making an Angel Altar

Although it is not necessary to have an angel altar in order to begin your workings with them, if you do set one up it quickly becomes an important part of your home. As you focus your attention on your altar, you might even start to see bursts of light around it, or have feelings of bliss while working there.

Choose the most appropriate place for you to do your angelic meditations and communications. It can be in your bedroom, living room, or really anywhere you feel most comfortable. Be sure to clean the area before you begin to set everything up.

The centerpiece can be either a picture or a statue of an angel that appeals to you. Remember, all the angels are connected to each other, so you can never choose the wrong image—just choose one that resonates with your heart.

The four elements of air, fire, water, and earth are sacred gifts that keep us alive. Therefore, when setting up an angel altar, we include these elements as precious offerings from our living planet. To represent air, you can use a feather or burn incense. A candle is fire, a container of water or a seashell is water, and a plant or a crystal is earth. When choosing objects for your altar, I recommend holding each one in your hands, closing your eyes, and asking, "Are you meant for my angel altar?" Then respect whatever the answer is, whether it comes to you as something you see, sense, hear, feel, or just know. Trust in your own way of receiving information.

Meditation:
Dedication of Your Altar to the Angels

This is to be the first meditation you do at your newly created altar. I suggest that to celebrate this occasion, you have an extra white candle and a red apple. As you begin, these two items are kept to the side. You will also want to have your journal and a pen handy to write down any impressions after the dedication is complete.

Light your main altar candle and the incense, if that is what you are using for the element of air. Pause before your altar with your eyes closed. Take three deep breaths, focusing your attention in the center of your chest. When you feel ready, face east and say, *I call to the Archangel Gabriel, and I ask you to come to bless my angel altar. Thank you for bringing me this new beginning.* Stand still for a moment and just listen, feeling into yourself for the presence of Gabriel.

When you feel ready, make a quarter turn to the right. You are now facing south. Say, *I call to the Archangel Raphael, and I ask you to come to bless my altar. I thank you for the light you bring that I might see my way clearly.* Stand still for a moment and just listen, feeling into yourself for the presence of Raphael.

When you feel ready, make a quarter turn to the right. You are now facing west. Say, *I call to the Archangel Michael. I ask that you come to bless my altar. Thank you for clearing the way for me and for protecting me as I go forward in life.* Stand still for a moment and just listen, feeling into yourself for the presence of Michael.

When you feel ready, make a quarter turn to the right, and now you are facing north. Say, *I call to the Archangel Ariel, and I ask you to come to bless my altar. I thank you for clear sight as I walk the path I have chosen.* Stand still for a moment and just listen, feeling into yourself for the presence of Ariel. When you feel ready, face your altar.

Pick up the apple and say, *This apple is a gift made from flowers, sunshine, rain, and wind, nurtured by the earth through the roots of the tree that grew it. This gift is made from everything sacred and is a token of my love.* Place the apple on the altar. Pick up the white candle and say, *I light this candle in dedication to the Light of Divinity within you and within me.* Light the candle and put it on the altar. Then say, *Ariel, Raphael, Michael, and Gabriel, I thank you for coming to bless my angel altar. I invite you to stay for as long as you would like. Thank you for blessing me and my home with your presence.*

Notice how you feel and write down as much as you can remember of what transpired during the ceremony. I predict that you will feel the energy of the archangels in your home for a long time. It's wonderful to leave the candle burning until it goes out, but do this only if it's safe to do so. Do not eat the apple. To complete the ceremony, you want to place the apple back into the natural world from whence it came. Therefore, after it has been on your altar for twenty-four hours, give it back to nature. Even in the city, you can find a tree to place it under, bringing the ceremony full circle.

Once the apple is returned to the earth, the ceremony is complete. You can now place things on your altar for angelic charging—for example, your jewelry or a gift you are giving to someone; be creative in using the sacred space you've made for the angels. The more you spend time before it, the stronger your connection to the angelic energies will become. You can also repeat the process of offering fruit, following the same procedure of returning it to the earth after twenty-four hours.

I predict that by spending a bit of time experimenting with the practice of automatic writing and/or by making an angel altar, you will find the angels beginning to connect with you in unexpected ways. They have limitless abilities to amaze as they bring us to joyful reunion with them.

God not only sends special angels into our lives,
but sometimes He even sends them back again
if we forget to take notes the first time!
—EILEEN ELIAS FREEMAN

CHAPTER 2

The Reunion with My Angel: How I Got to Where I Am

What follows is the story of how I came to be reunited with my angel, who, via automatic writing, has sent *you* a message laden with love. This message is especially for those who (like my former self) may be facing difficulty believing that angels are around them. Here is your message:

Please know that we (the angelic kingdom) are hoping you will have the desire to reach out to connect with this realm. We are all waiting to embrace your hearts and teach you about love by loving you more than you ever dreamed possible. All you need to do is decide to heed this call.

⁓

The reunion with my angel was a slow and sometimes painful process as my adult human ego encountered such divinity. The journey back to believing was not an easy ride for me.

I arrived at a center in Midtown Manhattan to begin my Reiki training. After checking in at the desk, I entered a room where about fifty other people were sitting in a circle of chairs. All of them were strangers to me. Fragrant candles were burning in the airy studio, and there was soft music playing as we waited for the Reiki master to arrive.

I had last-minute jitters and was very nervous. I worried that the training wouldn't work for me. My fears were reinforced as I looked around the room at my fellow students with their crystal necklaces, beads, and the like. *What am I thinking?* I wondered as I looked down at my blazer and jeans. *Am I the right kind of person for this?* I was already wondering how I was going to handle the embarrassment of not being able to "get" Reiki.

As the training got under way, the teacher recounted the story of Reiki, explaining how this healing practice had come forth in an enlightenment experienced by Dr. Mikao Usui. Though historical accounts vary from one source to another, Dr. Usui is often believed to have originally started out from a Buddhist monastery on a quest to uncover the ways in which the Buddha had healed with his hands. We learned that his search ended successfully twenty-eight years later when he was on a holy mountaintop close to Kyoto, Japan.

The story of Reiki was fascinating. After fasting and meditating on Mount Kuriyama for twenty-one days, Dr. Usui received a beautiful vision in which he was taught how to heal with his hands using spiritual power. He then named this system of healing *Reiki*, which in Japanese means "universal life force energy." In further explanation of the name, we were told that Reiki comes from the highest realms of the universe. We could call the source of its power whatever worked for us personally: God, Goddess, All That Is, and so on.

And so on? I wondered. I was very unsure as to what I wanted to call it.

With the history lesson behind us, we were next going to be led in a meditation to hopefully recreate some of what Dr. Usui had experienced by meeting a personal spiritual guide called a "Reiki master in spirit." This guide would help us understand our Reiki practice and would be a spiritual assistant in our future Reiki sessions. With thoughts of Japan, monasteries, and mountaintops in my head, I imagined the meditation would lead me to some sort of Buddhist helper.

I closed my eyes and followed my teacher's voice through all the steps that brought me to a room filled with golden light. In the very middle of the space, there was a very thick patch of mist, shrouding whoever or whatever was there to meet me. I felt waves of love washing over and through me and thought, *Oh, goodness, this is so strong. I must surely be imagining I'm in the presence of the Buddha!*

Much to my surprise, when the mist cleared, the one who stood before me was the angel I had communicated with in childhood! As I experienced pure shock, the angel rather lightheartedly conveyed the following thought: *Well, of course it's me. Who else did you think would be here?* I didn't know what to say! Whatever I was to experience there, I didn't expect it to have a sense of humor. After waiting a few moments, I asked for its name as directed by my teacher, but no name was given; only waves of love came to me.

After the meditation was over, we were assured that if we hadn't been given our Reiki master in spirit's name, it would be revealed to us one day in the future. *Yeah, sure,* I thought, chalking it all up to my theatrical imagination. How could I possibly believe in this stuff? By then, so many "real" things had happened in my life—I'd had a career as a legal secretary (talk about being grounded in this world!), gotten married, become a mother, watched the horrors of war and disasters on TV, lost my dear Gram to cancer, gotten divorced, struggled to be the best single mom I could possibly be, worried about bills, etc. There was just no time in my life for the "supernatural"!

Yet right after my Reiki training was complete, I began to spontaneously receive beautiful messages filled with love during my morning journaling, which was something I had been doing for years to handle all of the stress in my life. The grown-up me had stopped believing in spiritual things, and as I received these messages, I railed against the fate that seemed to be staring me in the face. I thought I must have been losing my mind from all the stress I was under.

The crack in my disbelief came at a health expo in New York City. It was 1997, and at that time not many people knew about Reiki. From the start of my practice, I had witnessed the tremendous powers Reiki has to heal the physical body, so I was devoted to bringing awareness of it to as many people as I possibly could. To that end, I rented a booth at the expo and was giving short Reiki sessions as demonstrations.

In the booth next to me was a kind young man. His name was Gerald, and he was at the expo doing aura photography. An aura is the energy surrounding one's body that is normally invisible to most people, but it can be photographed with a Kirlian camera. Years later, I would hear Dr. Mehmet Oz suggest this very same camera be used as a way to possibly prove the presence of energy medicine. Gerald asked if he could photograph my aura before and after I did Reiki on my first client of the day.

We did this little experiment and there was a stark difference in the before and after pictures. My aura in the before photo was certainly beautiful, very colorful in fact. In the photo taken after I had done Reiki, a huge, brilliant white light illuminated all the space above my head, shone down the left side of my auric field, and filled the center of my chest. Gerald identified this brilliant light as a being of very powerful love that was working with me. He recommended I do a little prayer to ask what its name was. He said it would help me work together with this being more fluidly if I knew what to call it.

Oh, what the heck? I thought. I turned to face the wall and whispered, "Please may I hear the name of my Reiki master in spirit today?"

The rush of business began and I forgot all about my prayer until I was in the depths of a Reiki session with a man who had come to my booth. With my eyes closed, I felt the swaying motion of the ocean beneath me as if I were standing on the deck of a boat (it turned out boating was his passion), when suddenly I heard the name "Archangel Gabriel." It shocked my eyes open! Until then I'd forgotten my request.

When there was a break in the action, I whispered to Gerald that I had heard a name. He excitedly sent me to the booth of a psychic at the other end of the hall to see if she could confirm the name of who was working with me. I had never in my life had dealings with psychics, so I had no idea what to expect. The woman was very normal looking and quite pretty with her amazing red hair and enormous, sparkling blue eyes. She was Irish and spoke with an accent. I asked if she could tell me the name of whatever spirit guide was helping me to do Reiki. I didn't tell her anything else at all.

The woman closed her eyes, took four or five deep breaths, and was very still for several minutes until she began to speak in a spectral voice unlike the one she had just been using. Her body jerked slightly as she spoke. "I am Gabriel. You feel my love. … You doubt that I am with you, but you will soon come to accept me, as we have known each other for a very long time and will continue to do our work together."

As the woman came out of her trance, I thanked her and, shaken, went back to my booth where Gerald was waiting for me with a little pin in the shape of the Archangel Gabriel.

A few days later, I was writing in my journal about my fears and anxieties, very upset about issues in my life. As I felt a shift in the air around me, I could almost hear the sound of wings opening. That's when the following transmission started coming through in automatic writing:

Just breathe ... and relax ... and let go! Invite pleasure into your life, into your reality, into you. Pleasure, pleasure, pleasure, for the world is certainly here for your enjoyment. Give yourself over to joy. Celebrate your life. Be happy. We will never abandon you. You have lessons to learn is all, and it is good. Why would we ever leave you when we love you so? Do not be afraid. We are here for you and we will catch you if you fall. Love, Gabriel

I'd encountered beautiful messages before, yet this was the first time I had such a profound physical experience beforehand, and the first time a name had been given as part of the transmission. But there it was again: "Gabriel." It was getting harder for me to deny, but even still, my ego held on. It told me I was just making it all up based on the crazy episodes from the health expo. Still, there was enough to make me wonder.

After that, I felt led to share the messages with my meditation students, and the results were incredible. People would often come up to me in tears after class, telling me that what I had said was exactly what they needed to hear—that the words brought them comfort, encouragement, and feelings of safety. But for me, although I was beginning to understand that these messages were coming from another place, I still couldn't believe they were from the Archangel Gabriel.

I must have very low self-esteem, I thought, *to think I need a guide like an archangel!* A big part of the problem for me was that these transmissions were coming through without effort. I felt they should be more difficult to receive if they were, in fact, coming from an angel!

As this new level of automatic writing started, my life began to reveal many pockets of darkness. I struggled day after day with feelings of worthlessness and failure. I was overwhelmed by fears on every subject and especially concerning my ability to contribute to the world in a meaningful way. I didn't realize it at the time, but I now believe that the touch of my angel had brought on a spiritual "healing crisis." Meaning things needed to get worse by coming out into the light, before they could get better.

I woke up one night with a start at 3:00 a.m. and was overcome by fear. I got up and began to write in my journal in order to calm down. Snippets of what I wrote were: "I am so terrified! ... It's frightening to feel so vulnerable and alone. ... I'm terrified of my future. ... I'm afraid I'm losing my mind and that there's really nobody out there. ... What will become of me? ... I feel I am standing on the edge of a cliff. If I look down, I am doomed. If I step out in faith, I just might be okay. It's risky. I feel that I can fall so far and crash and burn. That is my worst fear. ..." Then came:

You have only to concentrate on yourself. You are fine. Take what steps feel safe and lead toward what you need. Much is rising out of your life. Hold on and be patient. You will get to the other side of this, you will! This is a major shift and it hurts, but it's for the best. Stay focused on the present. Don't think too far ahead. Play more. Enjoy your days and your nights. Love, Gabriel

Soon after, one of my students handed me a book called *Interview with an Angel* by Stevan J. Thayer and Linda Sue Nathanson. From the first line I read of the transmissions Mr. Thayer had received from the Archangel Ariel, I cried. Here was someone who was *really* receiving information from an archangel, and the words felt like medicine to me.

As soon as I started reading *Interview with an Angel*, I was asked to call Mr. Thayer during one of my own automatic writings. *What? He'll never talk to me*, I thought. Nevertheless, more out of curiosity than anything else, I made the call. Much to my complete surprise, Mr. Thayer called me back and even scheduled a time to come visit.

As he came through my door and we shook hands, I found myself looking into the eyes of someone very calm and full of happiness, which immediately put me at ease. I felt reassured, and it was relaxing just to be in his presence. He had come to give me a session of a healing technique he had recently developed with the aid of the angels called Integrated Energy Therapy (IET). We set up my massage table in the living room and I lit candles and incense, and as I lay down, I felt happily serene. Thayer began the IET session, which was the wondrous transmission of energy using a gentle touch similar to Reiki.

As I lay on the table with the beautiful scent of frankincense wafting through the air, I felt like I was floating, and that's when Ariel arrived. Using Thayer's soothing voice, Ariel spoke about some personal matters that Thayer could never have known about. Soon after, with a sweetness that felt full of compassion, Ariel delivered a message that changed my life forever.

"The Archangel Gabriel is coming to you, and you continue to deny this to be so." With gentleness, Ariel continued, "Gabriel has chosen you to speak to because he knows you will make sure his loving messages are shared. Your efforts to reject him are egotistical." I was shocked! Ariel continued, "I ask that you look deeply within yourself and consider uniting with Gabriel. If you can find a way to do this, the results will bring love into the world."

These were the words that broke the ice of fear within me. Here I had been thinking it was egotistical to imagine an archangel was speaking to me, and Ariel was saying it was quite the opposite! Ariel's message melted my worries and opened my heart. From that moment on, I accepted the Archangel Gabriel as my Reiki master in spirit, my mentor, my protector, my guide, my partner with clients, and my helper with everything. I felt relief and joy as I opened to the love and grace of the angelic realm and to the peace and patience they exude. In that moment, I came to remember and accept the truth of the words that had been spoken to me as a child after my fall: *I am always with you, right by your side, helping you with your life.*

Meditation: Meeting Your Guardian Angel

Before we begin, I'd like to point out that angels aren't really male or female, yet for our convenience as humans, they usually have us experience them as one or the other.

You might like to put on some soothing music and/or light some incense, if that pleases you. Remember through all of the parts of the meditation as it unfolds, it doesn't matter if you see, sense, hear, or just know things as they happen. All the ways of experiencing your inner world are perfect—there's just your own unique way, which gets easier to embrace the more you do sacred work.

Sit comfortably, close your eyes, and notice your breathing. Bring your awareness into the center of your chest. See, hear, sense, feel, or just know your heart beating. Thank your heart for all of the wonderful things it does to keep you alive. Acknowledge your heart's connection to the power of divinity through its ability to love. Sit for just another moment, breathing easily in peace and gratitude.

When you feel ready, call golden light to surround you. And now, in the way that works best for you, let the golden light extend six feet in all directions—it goes through walls, the floor under your feet, and anything close by. The golden light holds you in a cocoon of safety. Relax into it and enjoy a moment of deep peace.

Now begin to imagine yourself standing at the base of a sturdy and beautiful tree. Gaze up and notice there is a low branch. Swing yourself up onto this branch. Climb upward into the upper branches of the tree. Take your time. Enjoy your connection to the tree and to the air as you climb.

When you get to the very top branches, a rainbow bridge appears before you. It leads out of the tree and slightly upward into a very large and brilliant orb of white light tinted with gold. You make your way across the bridge and enter the brilliant light.

Imagine yourself lying down, weightless in the light, resting. Before long, you begin to notice angels all around you, whether you sense, hear, feel, see, or just know they are there. Surrender into the love of the angels that surround you. Allow yourself to become ever more deeply relaxed with each passing millisecond by simply breathing.

Now in your vision, sit up. Pause for just a moment before you think, whisper, or say out loud, however it's best for you, *I ask my very own guardian angel to reveal yourself to me. I ask that you come to me in whatever way is best for me right now.* Then just sit peacefully, knowing that your guardian angel has been waiting for this very moment for a very long time. Be patient until your guardian angel begins to emerge from the light around you. Surrender to whatever happens in whatever way it does, without deciding how it's "supposed" to be. It can come slowly, or all at once; either way is powerful. There is no one way for this to happen. Your guardian angel will come to you in whatever way is best for you personally. Simply allow. Take your time and surrender to the experience, without rushing it at all.

Let your awareness open to the deep connection that already exists within your heart and mind between you and your guardian angel. This is a happy reunion with a very old friend. Take time to savor the experience of union. Notice as many things as you can. Let the love and peace of it wash through you. Take as long as you like, savoring it. If you wish, you can ask your angel to help you in solidifying the connection.

When you feel ready, ask your angel's name, or what it would like to be called. Wait to receive an answer and accept it in whatever way it comes to you. If no name is forthcoming at this time, you are welcome to spend time asking questions, if you wish. Most important of all, allow yourself to be washed in your angel's love.

When you are ready, say "thank you" to your angel for revealing itself to you as you rise and begin moving back toward the rainbow bridge. You can see it through the light. Pass out of the white golden light and onto the bridge. Cross the rainbow bridge, move back to the tree, and come all the way down into your body in the place where you have been resting.

Say "thank you" to yourself and to your guardian angel for this experience, as you welcome your spirit back into your body. Take three deep breaths, and as you do, enjoy being back in time/space. One, notice your fingers and toes. Two, feel yourself breathing. Three, open your eyes. Say "thank you" once again.

Write down in your journal as much as you can remember of what happened. Don't worry if you didn't get a name; you will know the name when the time is right. And remember, you can do this meditation as often as you'd like, and certainly whenever you wish to visit with your guardian angel for any reason!

Meditation for Your Heart's Desires (Or to Assist with a Crisis)
Part One: Acknowledge Your Crisis

Angels say that the time of martyrdom is over. That is old energy that no longer works on this planet. The new energy is about becoming an excellent receiver of the pure love that is Divinity—whether you call that God, Goddess, Source, or Universe—in order to shine your light as someone who exudes happiness. This is the kind of energy that will inspire others to turn away from judgment or hatred and turn toward love.

We have not been taught to fulfill our desires. In fact, we have been told throughout the ages that humans are bad and that we must sacrifice rather than be happy on Earth in order to make God love us. This old programming is very deep within the consciousness of the human race, so you must be patient with yourself. It may require more than one try to get in touch with even one thing that you really want.

The word *need* has a bad energy around it, and I have intentionally replaced it with the word *crisis*. Oftentimes, a crisis is caused by a deeper underlying wish that is being ignored. For example, I see this all the time with my breast cancer clients.

If everything is going along more or less smoothly for you in your life right now, then jump right to the meditation. However, if you are having a crisis, read on.

If you are having a crisis, when you get into the meditation and are addressing that, there is still the opportunity for your deeper heart's desire to begin to emerge. Therefore, before you even begin the meditation, take a moment to acknowledge to yourself that you will address the crisis and will allow the underlying heart's desire to begin to make its way into your awareness. Remember, it might take more than one try.

Part Two: The Meditation

I suggest you practice this meditation as much as you like. It's one that will never wear out its usefulness to you since the results build over time. Let your intention be that you will get in touch with, and fulfill, one of your heart's desires to start with. Fulfilling one desire gives way to another. Your desires are signposts along the road of your life that guide you to where you were always meant to be—the place you chose for yourself long before you were ever born into this world. This is why this meditation can be used over the course of your life.

You can record the meditation on any of your devices or have a friend read it to you. It can be done alone or in a group. If you find it helpful, light some incense or a candle and put on some music that you find soothing, but none of these things are necessary for you to have a wonderful experience of getting in touch with your heart's desires.

Sit quietly with your back straight or lie down. The experiences to come can be things you see, hear, sense, or just know; there is no "best" or "better" way for any of this to happen. There's just the way you are wired and how your inner world operates as the unique being that you are.

Bring your attention to the tip of your nose and notice the air going in and out as you breathe. Say "thank you" to the air, which automatically begins to raise your vibrations. Being grateful is the opposite of being a victim, so say "thank you" to the air for a moment or two. You may find other things rising up inside you that you are thankful for, and if you do, follow the experience to where it leads you.

When you feel ready to move on, imagine that your thanks transformed whatever you are sitting or lying on into a wonderful sea of kindness. Let kindness sink into your skin where you are touching the sea and allow it to run throughout your whole body.

Now give up the weight of your body and just float, weightless. Enjoy the freedom of just being in this moment of weightless enjoyment while you continue to fill up more and more with kindness. Enjoy the peace in your body, mind, emotions, and spirit. Rest.

Now as you continue to rest, call golden light to surround you, to flood your auric field, the field of energy around you that extends six feet in all directions. It goes through whatever you are resting on, through walls, floors, and furniture—nothing can stop the golden light from filling your aura. This is because you invited it to join you and you are a unique vibration throughout all of time and space. You are from the One Love, which is infinitely creating more and never duplicating anything it makes. So now the piece of God*dess* that you are is held in pure golden light, the light of the angelic realm.

The golden light affixes itself to the molecules of air you are breathing. Ask the angels to adjust your cells to their higher vibration of love as you breathe in the golden light. See, hear, know, or feel inside yourself becoming brighter, lighter, freer, and happier with each breath that you take.

Ask your guardian angel to come to your left side. This is because, as the angels have taught me, their energies and the energies of our spirit guides can easily flow into us from the left, because our left side is the "receiving" side of our body. Allow yourself to receive the inflow of your angel's energy; let it pour into you and flow through you all the way to your right side. Let yourself receive this internal bathing of angelic love. Rest in this joyful connection for a moment or two. Enjoy the divine love that is being given to you.

This is like using spiritual smelling salts. It wakes your spirit out of delusion and brings you out of being unconscious to your dreams. Let the love pour into you from your guardian angel for as long as you would like, or feel you need.

Begin to notice that a big ball of golden light is coalescing in the center of your chest. Notice that the ball of light gets larger with every passing millisecond.

Bring your awareness into the very center of that ball of light in your chest and ask yourself, "What is my heart's desire right now?" Just wait calmly without forcing anything. Let it rise out of your heart and into your awareness without judgment. Whatever it is, it is there for a good reason that will bring you another step forward in your life. Accept what you know as the current desire of your heart, and say "thank you." Say "thank you" to your heart, the golden light, and your own guardian angel for this wonderful awareness of what you now ask your guardian angel and all the angels to bring to you. Imagine that you are a sponge, absorbing the love and power of your desire. Absorb the love your angel and all of the angels have for you. Entrust the fulfillment of your desire to them.

Float. Rest. Communicate. Be.

Stay in this for as long as you feel comfortable, and when you feel ready, come back to normal consciousness. Write down as much as you can remember of what happened in your journal.

As I said, you can do this meditation as often as you like, even every day, if you want to. You may not be able to get in touch with a desire in the first go-round, but don't worry— you will eventually have success. It's just that we have been taught to deny ourselves by so many different things in society that our dream muscle has gone to sleep, but with practice, it will come fully awake again!

We should pray to the angels,
for they are given to us as guardians.

—ST. AMBROSE

Chapter 3

Angels as Guardians and Guides

There have been many times that the angels have kept me safe in ways I could never have predicted, or even imagined, beforehand. As I have continued to witness just how vast and deep the protection of angels can be, I have often been left speechless. Here are just a few stories of how Gabriel and the angels have protected me personally over the years.

Personal Angelic Assistance in Preparation for Reiki in the Operating Room

I have now witnessed many surgeries and medical procedures. I have even been in the operating room with Dr. Mehmet Oz during open-heart surgery. It was Gabriel who gave me the courage to go into an operating room in the first place, and to endure witnessing what may be the most violent kind of surgery performed in today's world.

When my client Susanna came to tell me she needed open-heart surgery within a week, she asked me to go with her. "Absolutely not," I initially said. "I get panicky in hospitals, and I can't stand the sight of blood."

However, during her Reiki session that followed, Gabriel whispered to me, "You must say yes to Susanna. There are many things that need to happen from this in the future. We will protect you; don't worry, just tell her yes and give her your résumé before she leaves." I thought it was a strange coincidence that I had composed a résumé of my Reiki work for the first time the day before her session. But following Gabriel's advice, at the end of the session I told Susanna I would do it if Dr. Oz agreed and sent her off with my résumé, hoping Dr. Oz would say no.

I was stunned when Susanna called me, bubbling over with excitement because Dr. Oz thought it would be a good idea to have me in the operating room. "He thinks it would be wonderful, since we already have such a strong working relationship. All he wanted to see was your résumé!"

There is always free will when it comes to working with angels, and just because Gabriel said there were things that would happen in the future, it didn't mean I had to do it. But I found that my desire to assist my client when she needed me the most, coupled with Gabriel's assurance that I would be protected, overrode my panic. So I spent the one week I had to prepare myself in meditation and prayer. I also called upon

Minh, a Reiki student whom I had trained to be a master. I asked her to come to my office to give me a Reiki session.

As I lay on the massage table with Minh's hands across the crown of my head, Archangel Gabriel's energy filled all the space around us, flooding the entire room with brilliant light. Gabriel took my hand, and the feeling of physical pressure was so strong I nearly sat up on the table. He began, "Don't worry, child, there is no need to be fearful; I'm right here, and I will be with you in the operating room as well." I was calm and peaceful as Gabriel continued, "During the surgery, you will be held in light more powerful than anything you've previously experienced."

Gabriel pointed out that I would be able to notice this more powerful light because many more angels would become active in the operating room at my request. His instruction to me was: *Even before the operation starts, silently call to the angels of Susanna and of the doctors and technicians, asking for their help. All those angels will then provide their light and love to assist in the surgery.* I began to drift off as he showed me a beautiful sword of angelic light that would be laid down next to Susanna on the operating table. I slept peacefully through the rest of the session and felt very calm when it was over.

I stretched after waking up at the end of the session and slowly sat up on the table to sip the water from the glass Minh placed in my hand. She began to tell me the incredible experience of what transpired for her during the session. I was fascinated by its connection to what I had seen and heard. Minh told me, "Since you are going into battle in the operating room, Joan of Arc came to lend you her sword. She infused you with bravery and told me you will be in powerful light." I didn't know quite what to make of these intertwined messages from the spiritual realm, but I was very touched by the emotion with which Minh conveyed her experiences to me. I bowed my head in acknowledgment of the blessings I felt.

Susanna's surgery did, in fact, go very smoothly, and the experience was extraordinary. Yet if not for the encouragement of Gabriel beforehand and the love of all the angels in the operating room, I would never have been able to endure such an extreme surgery with someone I love as much as I love Susanna. And as Gabriel had said from the beginning, many things were set in motion that continue even now to flourish in terms of blessings being available to patients at New York-Presbyterian/Columbia University Medical Center. The practice of having Reiki masters in the operating room is not present in any other hospital that I am aware of at this time. In the beginning, I was the only one who was going into surgery. Things have advanced now to where I lead a small team of Reiki masters I have trained who also assist patients during operations.

Angels Creating Physical Safety

Guardianship by angels can occur in so many different ways, and here's one that might be of a surprising nature.

With all the serious medical work I am called to do, it's very important that I have a place to go where I can renew myself spiritually—a place where I can forever open myself up to the infinite, ever-unfolding universe. That place for me is Glastonbury, England.

On December 20, 2012, I was in Glastonbury to celebrate the winter solstice, which coincided with the end of the Mayan calendar. I had gone to the office of Celtic shaman Jeremy White. In the middle of a healing ceremony he was conducting on my behalf, I silently called out to the angelic realm, "Gabriel, please help me find a safe place here in Glastonbury where I can begin to write about you and the angels."

When I left Jeremy's office, even though it was only early afternoon, it was practically dark outside. There had been pouring rain for days, so I put up my umbrella and marched out into the downpour, looking forward to snuggling under the covers in my room with a cup of hot tea at Little St. Michael's at the Chalice Well. As I began making my way up High Street, Gabriel whispered to me, "Go now to the Chalice Well gift shop." Following Gabriel's instructions, I sloshed my way through deep puddles and along slippery pathways until I finally arrived at the door.

A woman who was just leaving the shop held the door open for me as I entered. I was glad to get in out of the deluge. Allowing the warmth and gentle fragrance of the Chalice Well Healing Essences to soothingly wrap themselves around me, I savored the sensory experience as I placed my dripping umbrella into a stand by the door. I was already enjoying the pleasant energy that welcomed me and was immediately aware that I was the only customer in the shop.

Gazing over toward the shopkeeper's desk, my eyes connected with the salesperson. She looked at me with curiosity. I thought, *She must be wondering who in their right mind would decide to go shopping in such a downpour!* Nevertheless, after sharing polite greetings, we struck up an easy conversation.

She told me her name was Mascha and that she had moved to Glastonbury from the Netherlands. I was charmed by her European accent; her eyes sparkled with kindness as she asked me about my life in New York City. I found myself confiding in her, "I want to write a book about angels, and I'm praying that I can write it in Glastonbury."

Mascha looked at me very intently, and then she said, "Well, you could come and stay with me for that. You can write your book about angels at my house."

"Oh, do you have a bed and breakfast?" I inquired. (So many people in Glastonbury do.) "What do you charge?" (I was hoping she might have monthly rates.)

"Oh, no, I don't have any such thing. I just have my home with my beloved Karyn. As a matter of fact, she was just leaving as you were coming in and she held the door for you. You could come and stay with us, and there would be no charge."

I'm a woman from New York City, so that invitation shocked me into silence. I didn't know how to respond! I decided she was just being kind in some European way I didn't understand in order to encourage me. While I was pondering what to say next, Mascha had already turned away and was writing something down. I felt Gabriel's hand over my heart as she looked up from the desk and handed me a slip of pink paper.

"Here's my e-mail address," she said. "Let's keep in touch!"

When I got back to New York, Mascha and I began exchanging e-mails. Although it was solidified between us and

I now had a place to stay in Glastonbury, I still didn't have a book deal, which meant everything was definitely on hold. But whenever I turned on my computer to find another message from her, I would thank Gabriel for this miracle of love and kindness. Mascha often included photos of flowering trees in their garden, and once she even sent a photo of a rainbow she had taken that afternoon. Her accompanying message was, "We know you are coming! This rainbow is a faerie bridge for you to walk over."

I woke up at 5:30 a.m. one morning in February 2013 feeling like I needed to sit with my journal because Gabriel wanted to tell me something. I got up, padded out to my living room, and sat down on the sofa. I opened my journal and asked, "Gabriel, what's up? Why can't I sleep? I feel anxious—like energies are around me and inside me that are stirring. Why? Do you need to tell me something?"

What we wish to point out is, you are too concerned with issues that are without real merit—all is well. We will lead you "out" and into Truth as we see it, and the way to go. Relax and give over your cares to us. We see the road you are on and can lead the way. Hold out your hand to us—we are here.

I held up my left hand.

No one knows the way of your heart more than you. Your own "knowing" is based on your feelings—let yourself feel what you feel—notice the feelings and let them flow. Your

feeling apparatus is your doorway. Energy surrounds you.
Please close your eyes.

I closed my eyes. Gabriel and the angels brought me into
an incredible white golden light for a very long time, where I
knew everything was perfect. I was brought back to the moment in childhood when I had first encountered Gabriel and
relived the experience, hearing the words *"I am always here,*
helping you with your life."

Then I felt the energies around me begin to shift and am-
plify. Gabriel and all the angels began to speak together in one
voice. *Someone is coming! Someone is coming!* The energy got
stronger and stronger, until, much to my utter amazement,
I realized that Christ had come into my living room. Keep in
mind that I hadn't been raised in the Christian faith, and as an
adult I felt no connection to Jesus, so this was a very big shock
to me. Yet here he was, and he was so very kind and so full of
love.

He said he came to bring me home. I asked him, "Is it time
to die?" It felt so wonderful that I was happy to go if it were so,
yet underneath it all I could feel that I still had things to do.

"No, not yet. Not until you have everything. I will give you
everything, if you will hold out your hand to me." I knew I was
being washed in blessings. I knew I could ask for things, so I
asked to go to Glastonbury to write my book about angels. He
kissed my third eye and then anointed it with a touch of his
finger that I knew had the energy of sacred oil on it.

"I am always with you," he said. He stayed with me for a
while and then began to recede. As he did, I could hear the

angels singing and I could feel the difference within myself that his visit had wrought. Then Gabriel appeared in front of me saying, "The road will form before your feet. We are taking care of everything."

Soon thereafter, my agent read my book proposal and sent it on to the publisher of my previous book. On April 11, my book deal came through and I arrived in Glastonbury on April 30. On the day of my arrival, while moving my things into the beautiful little room in Mascha and Karyn's home, I rejoiced. With tears in my eyes, I thanked Gabriel and all the angels for taking care of everything and bringing me "home" to write my book. You are holding the results of angelic guardianship in your hands right now.

Angelic Family Blessings

After I had been a Reiki master for just four years, my brother David called me early on a December 1999 evening during the Christmas season. He let me know that our seventy-one-year-old father was missing in the woods in a remote area of northern Vermont. At the time, our parents lived very close to Canada, and earlier that afternoon Dad and a friend had gone walking in a forest preserve on the Canadian border. They had set out in different directions, intending to meet back at the car at 4:00 p.m. Dad hadn't come back when he was expected. His friend waited for him, but when the sun went down, he knew he needed to get help. A search party was now combing the dark expanse of the wilderness, looking for Dad.

"David, what could have happened?" I asked, full of dread as my brother tried to comfort me.

"Don't worry," he said. "Dad knows everything about how to be safe in the woods." But for me, that was exactly the point! Every one of us knew our dad was an expert outdoorsman. He practiced safety protocol better than anyone, so what in the world kept him from coming out of the forest when he was supposed to? My mind raced with terrifying possibilities.

David said, "Hey, just get on a train. I'll pick you up and we'll drive to Vermont together." Although he hadn't said it in so many words, we both knew our family was on the brink of disaster. Our mom and we six adult children had plummeted into the most primal of territories. The Rock of Gibraltar of our lives was missing, and none of us really knew what to expect from ourselves. The one thing we did know for sure was that we had to stick together to endure whatever was to come.

I was so upset I couldn't think of what to put in a suitcase, so my husband packed for me while trying his best to calm me down. As he was packing, he gently reminded me that I could project myself to wherever my father was, no matter how thick the woods. "Connect with him. You know you can. Give him your love and support."

Soon afterward I was on a train speeding toward Brewster, New York, a town just across the border from my brother's Connecticut home. I was barely aware of the lights of the passing towns as I stared out the window, but I could feel Gabriel surrounding me with love and comfort. I decided to reach out to my dad by writing him a letter.

"Dad, I love you so much. We all do. We're coming to find you," I told him. "Please be calm, Dad. I am asking the angels to be with you, and for you to be comforted by their light in the darkness." I continued to pour my love out to my father in that letter, and while I was writing to him, I felt our hearts connect, one to the other. When I closed my eyes, I could see him under a tree, and I felt love all around him. In my mind, I surrounded him with light.

David's wife and their daughter picked me up at the train station. David was back at home, packing, making arrangements to pick up our brother, Raymond, and staying in touch with our mom. When we got back to their house, David said that Mom had just called to say that the search had been called off for the night due to a shift in the weather. It was now raining in that corner of Vermont. This was chilling news. Dad would now be spending the night outside in the rain! Was he hurt? Could he find shelter?

When someone you love turns into a "missing person," it's hard to do the simplest things, and there are strange physical manifestations resulting from the strain. It felt to me like I was being shot out of a cannon, barreling nonstop toward a black hole of uncontrollable fear that would swallow me forever. I was looking out of my eyes, but I saw next to nothing. There was only longing and worry in every molecule of my being as I struggled to find my hope.

David and I picked up Ray, and we started the drive up to Vermont. This was a time when mobile phones were in their infancy, so none of us had one to use to stay in touch with Mom. But once I was with my brothers, things seemed a little better. It was easier for us to find hope by telling each other that everything would be fine. We even laughed when Ray said, "We'll probably get all the way up there, and Dad will be asleep in bed!" But our laugher was nervous, even while we hoped with all our hearts that it would be so.

As we got into Massachusetts, light snow started to fall. I tried to will it to stop. But the farther north we got, the harder it snowed. By the time we got close to our parents' home there was a raging snowstorm with high winds, the roads were treacherous, and the temperature was very low. We had to drive slowly, and I knew we were in trouble when my brothers, both notorious jokers, were totally silent in the front seat. The sound of the wipers as they dragged through the ice forming on the windshield scraped my nerves raw.

The snow was deep, and as we finally inched our way off the very last and northernmost I-91 exit in the United States, Ray expressed what we all felt when he suddenly blurted, "I wish it was me out there and not him!"

I started to cry. "What can I do?" I asked my brothers. "I want to go out to help find Dad if he isn't back yet." David and Ray took turns gently pointing out that I didn't have the proper outdoor clothing or boots, which could only lead to problems. They both told me I had to be strong. Since I was crying, I don't know which one of them finally said, "It's really best if you help look after Mom."

By the time we got to our parents' home, our sisters, Cindy and Donna, along with Donna's two boys, had already been there for about five hours. Sometime during the night, Scott, Donna's then fourteen-year-old son, told his mom that he wanted to go out to help find his grandfather. Donna had explained to him that it might not be such a great idea, because nobody knew what the searchers would find. She expressed the worry that his last memory of his grandfather might be bad if they found something tragic.

"Something bad could never be my last memory of Poppy," was Scott's reply.

It had taken my brothers and me much longer than the usual five hours to drive from Connecticut to our parents' house because of the bad weather. It was now 6:45 a.m. The minute we got in the door, Ray and David had to rush into their heavy clothes. A search party was waiting for them at the Derby State Police Barracks that included local rescue volunteers, the US Border Patrol, and the Vermont State Police. A bulletin had been sent out, and people were coming from all over New England to help locate Dad. The state police dispatcher had placed a call during the night to the New England K-9 Search and Rescue Squad. K-9ers from New Hampshire and Massachusetts with their valiant, highly trained dogs were already waiting at the barracks to participate in the search.

Donna told us that Scott wanted to go out with the search party to help find his grandfather. Since he had all the right gear, nobody had the heart to tell him no. So Ray, Dave, and Scott left, promising to somehow get in touch with us as soon as they had news.

Mom sat down on the couch and wrapped her arms around herself. After some time went by, it seemed like she wasn't even there. Stress can bring on all kinds of physical reactions so I asked her, "Mom, are you alright?"

"I'm holding your father to keep him warm," was her answer. Her concentration was intense, so we left her alone to do what she was drawn to do.

There was an unspoken vow between us that we would support each other by continuing to focus on thinking positive thoughts. But it was excruciatingly painful whenever any stray thoughts of what *might be happening* slipped in.

While this was going on in Vermont, we kept in touch by phone with our sister, Sharon, who lived in Colorado. Sharon was held in the circle of love and support created by friends who had rushed to her side.

As for me, I kept tapping into the light to try to keep myself calm while asking the angels to guard Dad. The demon of doubt sat on my shoulder, waiting to devour me at any sign of weakness. Five minutes seemed like hours. Whenever I looked at Dad's empty slippers by the door, I got a lump in my throat and had to quickly look away from them. The temperature continued to drop as the snow fell, whipping across the windows in the thirty-mile-an-hour winds.

Our dad ... had he fallen? Was he conscious? Was he frightened?

At around 8:30 a.m., I was shaking apart. The weather was getting worse. The winds were howling outside the house. Survival was becoming less and less likely. I took myself out of earshot to call my husband from the downstairs phone. The minute I heard his voice, I started to sob. He said he knew where Dad was—he'd seen him while meditating. Dad was close to a road near a bridge.

"They'll find him," he said. "Try to stop crying, okay? You have to be strong for your mother." As I listened to the raging wind, I asked him, "Please promise me that Dad will come back to us!" Of course he couldn't promise me that, but I still had to get myself to stop crying. Once I was able to stop, I hung up the phone and went back upstairs.

As the Audubon Singing Bird Clock chirped its bird songs with each passing hour, we got more and more discouraged. Why weren't we hearing something? When Mom went to take a quick shower, Cindy lamented how Dad had certainly been soaked in the pouring rain before this awful snowstorm blew in. He must have frozen after getting wet.

Once Mom was done with her shower, she went back to hugging herself on the couch. It was heartwrenching to watch her. Cindy jumped up, saying, "I'd better go clean the snow off my car in case we have to leave in a hurry." Donna and Jeffrey went out to help her. As I looked out the window, I could see Cindy and Donna crying hysterically while they pushed the snow off Cindy's windshield. Up until then, none of us had cried in front of each other. We felt it was our solemn duty to stay strong for each other.

Now that we were alone, Mom started to weep broken-heartedly. "Oh my God, where's your father? He's been out in this weather far too long. How could he possibly still be alive? I'm so scared! What are we all going to do? How will we ever manage this?" She cried wretchedly while I held her and rubbed her back. But she stopped crying the moment she heard the returning footsteps of Cindy, Donna, and Jeffrey on the porch.

The events of that morning are scrambled in my mind, but I remember Donna and Jeffrey starting to make bread. Being too young to go out looking for his granddad, Jeffrey did his solemn best to be a comfort to us. As he and his mom mixed the flour and all the other ingredients together, with as much enthusiasm as he could muster under the circumstances, Jeffrey said, "Don't worry. Poppy will come back when the bread is ready."

That sent me over the edge. I knew I wasn't going to be able to keep myself from crying any longer, so I blurted out, "Well, it's my turn. Time to take a shower!"

With that I flew into the bathroom and turned all the taps on full force. The sound of the streaming water covered my sobs. I began to whisper what was in the depths of my soul. I knew my father wasn't going to be coming back. "Gabriel," I pleaded, "please help me to endure the tragic and unexpected loss of my father."

I was too upset to hear any words from Gabriel, but I felt calmness wash through me.

By 10:30 a.m., we were cracking even more under the strain. Mom asked that we join hands and pray together. We closed our eyes and prayed with emotion. Then Mom moved back to her spot on the couch, concentrating on holding our father again. The time dragged by while we tried not to listen to the howling wind.

Close to noon, because none of us had eaten anything since the afternoon before, we decided to put butter on the now freshly baked bread. I was holding a knife full of butter when the phone rang. The knife clattered to the counter as I dropped it, running to put my arms around Mom. Donna ran to hold her from the other side, while Jeffrey knelt in front of her, holding his grandmother's hands.

Cindy answered the phone. Mom was sitting up, stiff as a board, unable to even breathe. She looked awful. Then everything happened very quickly. We could hear Cindy say, "No, this is her daughter." Then she burst into tears and I couldn't breathe, trying to hold Mom up as she slumped over in collapse. "Oh my God! They found him walking in the woods, and he seems to be all right!"

We all screamed. In a flash, everything in life shifted gloriously. In that one instant, I saw my mother's face change from a broken old woman into that of a young girl who would be reunited with her beloved.

Since his sons and grandson had been in another part of the forest when he was found, Dad had gone in an ambulance with the EMS team only. When we got to the hospital, the emergency room doctor was giving him a thorough check-up. Even though he had fallen into a swamp and all his clothes had turned to ice on his body, Dad had no frostbite; he didn't even have a scratch. The doctor told my parents that he couldn't explain why Dad, at age 71, was in such great condition after all he had been through.

I have my own opinion about what transpired in the woods that night, but the logical explanation Dad gave to us was that his ceaseless fascination with nature had caused him to lose track of time. He described coming upon a large grove of trees with marks in the bark high up on their trunks and realized he had stumbled upon something special. It was a place where the enormous bull moose of the forest had come together to scrape the velvet off their horns. Dad was having a marvelous time pondering the size of the creatures, held in the thrall of this natural wonder. He had inadvertently lost track of time.

After realizing he wouldn't make it back to the car by the appointed hour, he still tried to find his way out of the forest. In the dark, he fell into a swamp and decided he'd better stop moving around in the pitch dark before he fell and broke a bone. Once he stopped, he could see lights, so he knew people were looking for him, and that gave him the strength to survive the night, in spite of the blizzard. He found a big tree and spent the night with his face up against it, using it as shelter as much as he could against the wind. The tree was near a bridge close to a road, just as my husband had seen in his meditation vision. Dad grabbed what warmth he could by wrapping himself in a space blanket given to him more than thirty years before that he unfolded from his pocket.

But that's not the end of the story. Within the first few weeks of January 2000, a Vermont State Police trooper came to interview Dad to ask him which techniques they used in the search had worked the best. They don't always get the chance to ask these questions, because not everyone they find has survived, especially in winter. The officer had a checklist, and Dad was giving his answers to rate the value of each thing they had done during the search.

When the officer was through with his questions and was closing his notebook, Dad had one more thing to say. "Officer, I really do appreciate every single thing that you and the other rescuers did, but do you know what was the most effective? It was when you had all those vehicles drive out to the edge of the ridge. When I saw the whole ridge lit up, I knew people were looking for me and it helped me to live through the night. I wanted to be alive in the morning when you got to me."

There was a long pause while the officer looked at my dad, trying to gauge his seriousness. "Mr. Somers," he finally said, "we never did any such thing. We never drove vehicles up onto the ridge, and we never lit anything up. The fact is, we had to give up the search early, when the rain started. That's when we all went home. We couldn't begin the search again until the next day when the sun came up."

My dad, "Mr. Sensible," a real $1 + 1 = 2$ kind of guy, didn't know what to make of that. But when he looked into the eyes of the state trooper, who had no doubt witnessed many things in his police career, my dad began to realize that something extraordinary had happened. He didn't know what it was and wasn't ready to try to figure it out, but for me, it was proof. Proof that Gabriel and the angels had been the light in the darkness that gave Dad the courage to live.

I will now give you two meditations. One is to formally ask your guardian angel to stay active around you, guarding you always. The other is for use in emergency situations, where someone you love needs help, or if you are worried about someone you love under any circumstances.

Meditation: Asking Your Guardian Angel to Always Be There for You

You can record the following meditation on any of your devices, or have a friend read it to you. It can be done alone or in a group. If you find it helpful, light some incense or a candle and put on some music that you find soothing, but none of these things are necessary for you to activate your angel as a full-time guardian.

Sit quietly with your back straight, or lie down. The experiences to come can be things you see, sense, hear, or just know; there is no "best" or "better" way for any of this to happen. There's just the way you are wired and how your inner world operates as the unique being that you are.

Bring your attention to the tip of your nose and notice the air going in and out as you breathe. Say "thank you" to the air, and continue with that, which automatically begins to raise your vibrations. Being grateful is the opposite of being a victim, so say "thank you" to the air for a moment or two. You may find other things rising up inside you that you are thankful for, and if you do, follow the experience to where it leads you.

When you feel ready to move on, imagine that your thanks transformed whatever you are sitting or lying on into a wonderful sea of kindness. Let kindness sink into your skin where you are touching the sea and allow it to run throughout your whole body.

Now give up the weight of your body and just float, weightless. Enjoy the freedom of just being in this moment of weightless enjoyment while you continue to fill up more and more with kindness. Enjoy the peace in your body, mind, emotions, and spirit. Rest.

Now as you continue to rest, call golden light to surround you, to flood your auric field, the field of energy around you that extends six feet in all directions. It goes through whatever you are resting on, through walls, floors, furniture—nothing can stop the golden light from filling your aura. This is because you invited it to join you and you are a unique vibration throughout all of time and space. You are from the One Love, which is infinitely creating more, and never duplicating anything it makes. So now the piece of God*dess* that you are is held in pure golden light, the light of the angelic realm.

The golden light affixes itself to the molecules of air you are breathing. Ask the angels to adjust your cells to their higher vibration of love as you breathe in the golden light. See, hear, know, or feel inside yourself becoming brighter, lighter, freer, and happier with each breath that you take.

Call to your guardian angel. It doesn't have to be out loud; you can do it silently if you prefer. Your angel always hears your thoughts when you are reaching out to it.

Say or think to it, *I ask that you guard me always. You have my permission to take care of me, even when I don't know I need*

protection. Thank you for always being there for me from now on.
Offer your dominant hand, palm facing upward, so that your
angel can press its energy into your palm. Enjoy any sensations you have for as long as you like. Then with a "thank
you," take a deep breath and let yourself come back. Notice
your body, just where you are. Take three deep breaths to
bring your awareness fully back into your body.

Meditation: Activating Guardian Angels in Emergency Situations

When an emergency is under way, there is very little extra energy available with which to concentrate on setting up a meditation. What you need is a way to take immediate action.

If there is a crisis in your life of any kind involving yourself or anyone you love, ask your guardian angel for immediate aid by saying whatever is in your heart. For example, *Dear
Guardian Angel, please activate Archangel Michael and all the angels that can help me right now. Thank you, thank you, thank you.*

If someone you know or love is in any kind of trouble, you
can say, *I ask that the Archangel Michael protect (insert name). I ask
that my guardian angel connect with the guardian angel of (insert
name) to activate the highest light of pure love around (him/her/
them). Please take care of me by taking care of (insert name). Thank
you, thank you, thank you.*

Obviously, in an emergency situation you might have things that you must do, but don't worry. The angels get busy the minute you ask for their help. You can check back in with them whenever it is appropriate for you.

Angels descending, bring from above,
Echoes of mercy, whispers of love.
—FANNY J. CROSBY

CHAPTER 4

Angels in Reiki

After I came to accept that Gabriel was really in my life, I began to wonder just how I was to proceed, and what I was supposed to do about it. Up to that point, everything he had said to me seemed to indicate that I was to ... *what?* Was I being entrusted to deliver messages to people, and if so, to whom? Or was there something else more urgent that needed to be done? My heart was on fire to put inspiration into action.

Since Gabriel had started to make his presence known to me when I began my Reiki training, I decided the first logical step I could take toward building my own awareness and happiness was to devote myself to my work as a Reiki master. As I've shared the love inherent in Reiki with those who've come through my office door, Gabriel has always been there to guide me. Reiki was, and continues to be, a powerful doorway through which angels have made themselves known to my clients as I've worked on them.

What follows are a few stories from different times in my practice as I've devoted myself to my Reiki clients. It will help you to understand the full impact of not only involving oneself in this type of healing modality (whether as the practitioner or client), but also what it means to welcome angels into your life.

Calling In the Angels

Whenever I start a Reiki session, I get the angels involved right away by saying an opening prayer. I usually say the prayer out loud unless speaking is inappropriate, in which case I do it silently. I've recited a version of this invocation since the beginning of my practice, so you can be sure that every session you read about started with a request for help from the angelic realm before Reiki was ever administered.

Here's how it goes more or less each time: *I call to the highest of spiritual beings of infinite light and unconditional love. I ask that you join us now and that you seal us in a circle of light and love. I ask to connect with my Reiki master in spirit, the Archangel Gabriel, to my higher self, to the angel and higher self of (my client's name), and to any other angels and spirits from the highest realms of light who would like to assist in this healing session. I give thanks for your presence and thank you in advance for all of your help.*

Angels Confirming Life Path

A client named Chelsea came to me after hearing from a friend of hers just how powerful his Reiki session had been.

Chelsea didn't have any pressing problems; she was mostly just curious to see what Reiki would be like for her.

I put on soothing music and got Chelsea settled on the table. I was happy to see that she immediately relaxed. She fell asleep almost as soon as I finished the last words of the opening prayer.

The Reiki practitioner has one experience while the client has another, and this is completely normal. In this case, at the very start of Chelsea's session while she was already sound asleep, I held my hands across the crown of her head and with my inner sight I saw a Y. This indicated to me that Chelsea was currently standing at a crossroad in her life.

As I asked Gabriel about this, he told me that Chelsea was facing a career change and whatever she decided to do would be fine in the big picture—any decision she made would result in forward movement because her life was already on the fast track. *Chelsea is very protected, yet if she is able to choose a career path that she feels connected to in her heart, she will advance even quicker.* Gabriel's message was clear. *No matter what Chelsea may choose to do in the immediate future, she will be guided to her highest good.*

While continuing to hold my hands in place across her crown, I could feel her spiritual growth was evolving at a rapid rate of speed. The present spiritual awakening was being influenced by a past life that I was next shown. I saw Chelsea in what felt like the Spanish Inquisition, turning on some sort of wheel, very close to death. In that lifetime, she was a person who had a strong connection to and communication with angels. However, it was not acceptable by the religious authorities at that time for regular, everyday people to be in touch with angels, so she was being tortured. I somehow knew that even though her body had been broken, her tormentors had never broken her spirit.

I felt a residue of that lifetime's torture and in a flash everything switched to Gabriel uniting with me to send Reiki into Chelsea's physical body to do whatever needed to be done to eliminate the past trauma. Chelsea continued to sleep through everything.

I received confirmation of what I had seen during the session after Chelsea woke up. While sitting on my table, sipping the water I had given her, she told me she was making decisions about a job change and that she wanted to change all aspects of her life along with it. Chelsea confided how she was feeling herself gravitating toward leading a more spiritual life and was trying to figure out how she could earn her living in a way that would give her more access to the spiritual part of herself. She also mentioned that she had dreamed during the Reiki session that she was in the presence of a powerful being of light who had blessed all the different parts of her life.

I found out later that after her Reiki session she left her job and was beginning her studies to be a minister.

Angelic Help for Child Abuse Trauma

I was very happy to receive a new Reiki client named Katrina, a beautiful and talented artist. As I shook her hand in greeting, I felt a rush of sadness pour through me. I wondered what had happened in her life that left such a powerful energy of unhappiness within her.

Katrina and I started out by talking so she could get comfortable with me. We sat opposite each other in my cozy office as she began to open up, explaining that she had experienced a particular unhappiness in childhood.

"My parents divorced when I was very young," she explained. "My mother was very loving and supportive, but my father remarried a woman who was mean to me, and the relationship with my father became strained after his new marriage."

The tale she told was a sad one. Katrina described growing up in the home of her loving mother, with trips to visit her father that were traumatizing because of her very abusive stepmother. Her stepmother was apparently like something out of a bad fairy tale.

"Whenever I visited my father, I had to live under the iron rule of my stepmother, who was very cruel to me. She always told me that I was bad and stupid. And she left notes around the house telling me I was fat and ugly and that I needed to change everything about myself."

Gabriel now whispered to me, "Even as a child, Katrina was always very beautiful. That's why her stepmother couldn't open her heart." Because angels speak in the language of love, those were the only words Gabriel could use to tell me Katrina's stepmother was jealous of her.

Katrina shared the wish of what she had longed for ever since she was a little girl. She wanted to know that her father loved her, explaining that he had never expressed the love she so desperately needed since the divorce of her parents. This had only compounded the effects of having a mean step-mother; Katrina always felt that her father put her stepmother's needs ahead of hers. All these things together had created an inner imbalance with serious effects she was suffering from as a young adult.

The child within felt she was somehow unworthy of her own father's love. Katrina's negative imprinting left her feeling like she had to punish herself for not being perfect enough to be loved by her dad. Consequently, the young woman she had become was afraid to eat; she was bone thin, nervous, and suffering from an ever-weakening physical constitution brought on by her own self-neglect.

"All this is being imposed on her by the child within who always wanted love," Gabriel whispered to me. Katrina was unaware she was punishing herself for something that had never been her fault.

Angels can help those of us who have been abused as children. A young child instinctively knows they are dependent upon their parents to survive. An abused child often feels like something must be wrong with them and that they themselves are responsible for the abuse. Most of the time, the automatic response is a belief that the parents must be right, so the only answer is to find what needs to be fixed and fix it in order to be loved. "Maybe if I'm better, smarter, faster, thinner … then they will love me."

As she lay down on the pink sheets of my table, with her long, dark hair streaming out around her face and across the pillow, her beautiful blue eyes looked up at me sadly until I asked her to close them. I put a lavender-scented eye pillow over her eyes and opened the session, calling to Gabriel, my higher self, Katrina's higher self, and to her healing guides and angels.

The immediate response I felt of the Reiki energy pouring through was accompanied by the presence of powerful spirits all around us, including those of her deceased great-grand-parents. Without speaking out loud, I asked Gabriel and all the angels to help with shifting the negative patterns of self-torture out of Katrina that abuse had created within her.

When I had my hands across the top of Katrina's head, I was asked to speak to her. "The Archangel Michael is here. Michael is offering to remove from your mind and even from your cells the residue of all the things that have caused you to hurt for so long," I said. As directed, I continued, "Please take a moment to ask Archangel Michael to take this stuff out of you. By asking him for his help, you give him your permission to help you." In the moments that followed, I could feel huge shifts taking place within her.

After about ten minutes, Michael let me know that some of the patterns were very deeply embedded, and he told me what to do. As directed by Michael, I said to her, "It's going very well, Katrina. To make it work even faster, from your heart but without speaking words out loud, keep thanking Archangel Michael for doing this for you." I could feel the difference immediately as she followed that direction, sensing an ever-deepening release of the past, with things pouring out of her, things that were whisked away by bands of angels.

"Thank you" was the powerful tool that united Katrina's heart with Archangel Michael, thereby intensifying her ability to let go and enabling Archangel Michael to work *with* her to lift the negative imprints out in a stronger and faster way. As Katrina continued to thank Archangel Michael, she began to cross over into the realization that she deserved to be loved, to be free and happy in her life.

I was next told to ask Katrina to "float in golden light and call to your own guardian angel." I continued speaking the instructions I was hearing. "Ask your guardian angel to lie down on your left side, because that side of you is open to receive an immediate inflow of your angel's love. Allow all the hurts Archangel Michael is lifting out of you to be replaced by the divine love flowing into you from your angel." The experience of being cleared and filled up with love was so strong that Katrina cried. It was a joy for me to witness just how much love, care, and blessings were surrounding sweet Katrina.

At the end of the session, the transformation was visible to me as Katrina sat up. I encouraged her to continue working with Archangel Michael and her own angel at night when she lay down to go to sleep. The instruction was to ask Michael to remove anything she had picked up from the day and to summon her guardian angel to her left side before falling asleep, since new energy moves in from the left. What went unsaid was that Michael would continue to remove anything still remaining inside her from her past bad experiences with her stepmother.

Angels Healing from a Distance

A good portion of my Reiki healing work these days is done remotely using a special long-distance technique. I love offering distance Reiki because I can be anywhere and do a session for someone in a completely different part of the world. Although the basic core of my distance healing sessions has remained the same, with the help of Gabriel, new aspects have developed over time.

For distance sessions, I frequently have no connection to the client, meaning most of the time I've never met them. I haven't even seen a picture of them and I have no idea what their life is like. They may or may not tell me what they want from the session. But it doesn't matter either way. In the end, the Reiki will deliver whatever the client needs.

These days, I sit with a journal and a pen, because I get messages for people as I do their remote healing sessions. Gabriel is always teaching me new things about healing, and while he is directing me to do certain procedures during each session unique for the person, he's also the one who gives me messages for the client. This is why my writing journal is a crucial part of the remote healing sessions that I do.

I've developed a shorthand that enables me to write down a quick word or phrase to remind me of the full message given by Gabriel. For example, during a recent session I wrote down the words "chaos, waterfall (of emotions), worry, seeking peace, body pain, danger, go home for a while, uneasiness, ask the angels to be with you to open the way, ask for what you want from angels and people." Words and phrases like these then lead me to give a full explanation of what Gabriel had to say to them specifically.

I spoke to a client right after her session to discuss the messages and to let her know what else had transpired on my end during the hour. She sent me an e-mail within a week to let me know how much things had changed and how much better everything was for her. She was now on her way to visit her family in her home country and her romantic relationship had begun to tremendously transform.

In another session that had profound effects, I wrote down: "Too many thoughts, relax and trust; allow hope; turn away from worry. Since doctors can't find anything wrong, it's time to allow yourself to be well—to replace fear with belief. ... Daily give yourself permission to release any limitations from the past and the present, then call Archangel Michael to assist you in that releasing. Ask Archangel Gabriel to change it to something positive. Sleep enfolded in angel wings. Say 'thank you.'"

In this case I sent an e-mail, and I was contacted immediately afterward, letting me know that after months of not being able to sleep, this client was now sleeping like a baby!

The messages from Gabriel during distance sessions pass through the whole of the angelic realm. Since the person receiving the Reiki has at least one guardian angel, and their angel and Gabriel are in direct communication, the messages flow through, empowered by all the angels there are.

The client often feels the presence of the angels, sometimes even in a physical way during their session. For example, one client felt her face washed in warmth and another felt like someone was holding his hand. This is very profound for the clients: the messages I deliver after the distance session, either via e-mail, Skype, or phone, really hit home.

I had a request for a healing session from someone in London who had injured her leg and needed a quick healing in order to do a bicycling fundraiser event called Ride Across Britain. It's so interesting how things go—when there is a particular issue at hand, even deeper healing is administered during a distance session due to the powerful insight of angels.

Archangel Gabriel and I worked together with her own guardian angel to bring balance into her whole being to stimulate her courage to keep going in the face of such a threat to her dream. During the session, Gabriel said to me, "We are bringing balance to both of her legs, because her right leg has been working doubly hard to make up for the left leg's injury." At the very end, Gabriel, her guardian angel, and I all worked over her beautiful heart to activate her connection to her own angel and to stimulate her courage in the face of her obstacle.

When I heard back from her about a month later, she reported that she had recovered fully. She was able to make the Ride Across Britain, which she said was one of the most amazing experiences of her life.

In another of my distance Reiki sessions, I was taught a procedure that I now incorporate into my distance Reiki work. The person I was working on happened to be one of my Reiki students. Since we already had such a strong connection with each other, I didn't have to go through the steps of setting up a spiritual connection to her energy. This being the case, and it being the right time (I might add), it was easier for Gabriel to show me this new technique.

As I was approaching the last fifteen minutes of the session, I felt my hands guided up to encircle my client's energy field. The field of energy, or aura, around her was then flooded with the golden light of the angelic realm. I felt Gabriel step inside my body, and I channeled the pure love of the entire angelic realm through me and into my client's energy field. As if she was right in front of me, I saw the golden light seep into my client's skin. It was stunningly beautiful, and really, there are no words to describe it!

When I was close to finishing this book, a new client reached out to me who had been a student at Columbine High School at the time of the shooting. He asked for a distance Reiki session. As the session got under way, many angels came to work with me and they told me that the client was standing at the crossroads. Gabriel advised that the client could ask his guardian angel and the archangels to form a path before his feet.

"Tell him not to worry," Gabriel said. "Tell him to ask us for our help, and then he can just step out on the path. It's time for him to start receiving blessings, rather than be stuck in the fear that everything will be snatched away." The angels formed a picture for me inside my mind, showing me how he was feeling guilty for having survived. Gabriel whispered to me, "He keeps asking himself, 'Why didn't it happen to me?'" The remedy came in a direct message I was to give to my client. "It's time to give up that worry. You have work to do on the planet Earth, and being stuck in guilt is hurting you," said Gabriel. "To honor those you knew who died, please connect your heart and soul to what you came to Earth to do. We will help you, if you will but ask."

The fact is, we are all worthy of love. The angels want us to know that we deserve to flourish, no matter what we may have witnessed or survived. No matter what may have happened in our past, the angels can help us get on the right track so we can be happy again and live a fulfilling life. All we ever have to do is ask.

Angels, Trauma, and PTSD

I can never predict what the angels will do to help those who come to me for healing. The following case was a complete surprise.

A tall, handsome Marine with dark blond hair and piercing blue eyes came to my office all the way from California in the hopes that I might be able to help him with his posttraumatic stress disorder (PTSD). As a commanding officer of a high rank, Bob had been deployed to Afghanistan four times. At the suggestion of a friend, he had read my first book, which talks about the benefits of Reiki for PTSD.

In our conversation before his session, as if discussing something as casual as the weather, Bob began to quietly tell me the most horrific things imaginable. He showed me a silver bracelet he wore with the names of two dear friends engraved upon it; he had viewed these friends' bodies after they had been tortured and killed. He told me he had nearly lost his own life on three separate occasions, including once when his entire convoy had been blown up by improvised explosive devices (IEDs) that detonated one after the other as he watched until the vehicle he was in exploded as well. He talked to me about what it was like to wonder if he was dead.

Bob told me he didn't trust anyone around him with the news that he had PTSD. His overwhelming fear was if "they" found out, his command would be stripped from him, he would be put on drugs, and he would be thrown out of the military. He was hoping I could help him, because he didn't want to leave the Marines—in fact, he felt he wanted to return to Afghanistan to help those he had left behind.

"Angels, please help," I silently implored as I listened to his tales.

When Bob finally got onto the table, I covered him with a green sheet and an extra blanket. I opened my heart and asked Gabriel to come fill me with the energy of angelic light and love; then I performed the usual opening prayer. In this case, I called in the Archangel Michael along with Bob's own guardian angel to assist Gabriel and Michael.

When I call upon the Archangel Michael, I ask him to use his powers to very precisely lift out the energies of things that need to be eliminated, so that Gabriel has space to pour in the healing light of divine love, which brings about the new changes. I could see in my mind's eye a sparkling golden light all around Bob and could feel Michael and Gabriel spinning energies within him in two opposite directions, Michael clearing and Gabriel stirring in the restoration. At the same time, I felt a powerful transformation happening for Bob in his physical body as Reiki poured through me and out of my hands.

When the session was over, Bob remained very still on the table, and although he talked to me, he wasn't really awake. "How are you, would you like some water?" I asked.

"No thanks, ma'am. I'm fine," he said. After more than five minutes went by, he still hadn't moved a muscle. He was like a block of stone, with the lavender-scented pillow still covering his eyes.

All of a sudden, Bob began to cry out, "We need some protection here!" He lifted his arm and pointed. "Go over there and protect those guys!" I knew I had to follow what he asked me to do, so I raced over to the window at the northwest corner of my office where he had indicated and held up my palms. In front of the window stood two spirits. I could see the fire escape and the buildings across Broadway through their bodies, and I knew the men standing there were the friends from Bob's bracelet.

With my palms up, I sent Reiki to the two spirits while I whispered to Gabriel and to the guardian angels of the men standing before me, "Please! Help! Gabriel, dear angels, please help these spirits!" In a split second, the men were surrounded by golden-white light. I felt the men responding quickly to the powerful love that washed over and through them, and I watched as they surrendered their anguish, transforming into light in the presence of the angels who had come to bring them home.

Just before the spirits left with the angels, they gave me a message for Bob. "Tell Bob we are grateful to have had him for a friend and as our commanding officer during our time together. Please let him know that we are safe." I watched the golden-white light around them grow brighter and brighter. Just before they disappeared, the light intensified in one final surge, absorbing them completely, and then in a flash, the light was gone. The Marines had gone home.

Another ten minutes of complete silence passed before Bob finally stirred on the table. Once he was fully awake, I helped him to sit up and I explained what had happened. He was stunned. "I pointed, and I spoke out loud?" "Yes." He had no recollection of any of it. With emotion, he queried, "My friends were in front of the fire escape?" "Yes." "The *fire escape*?" he asked again. I saw his eyes fill up with tears before he bowed his head so I wouldn't see, and I understood the significance that escaping fire held for him. When I conveyed the messages from his friends, he looked up at me and nodded to let me know he understood.

There are so many people out there who have been traumatized by war and by other things as well. Once PTSD takes hold, it can tear families apart, because it is passed on to others. There is even a name for it, "secondhand trauma." The fact is, anyone can ask the angels for help, not just me on their behalf in a Reiki session. All *you* ever have to do is call on angels for assistance. They are there for anyone who asks. Angelic healing is something more powerful than words can ever say and is something that you can do for yourself, just by

within, so let yourself have the whole experience;
back.

e angels to help you. Ask them to break the bonds—
at are inside you—connecting you to this past event
e other experiences surrounding it. You deserve to be
o be healed. Cry, scream, get it all out into the open.
ng as you need. See, hear, sense, feel, or know when
s come to break the bonds. Let everything go with
it be complete and acknowledge that everything is
aying "thank you" to the angels for the healing.

on as you feel able, bring the paper with your writ-
to a place to safely burn it. As it burns, send a bless-
your heart to the One Love and give thanks for your
sformation.

you are ready, sit with your journal and your guard-
Write down what happened and what it means to
may not remember it later and will want this record
elf.

his physical body as Reiki poured through me and out of my
hands.

When the session was over, Bob remained very still on the
table, and although he talked to me, he wasn't really awake.
"How are you, would you like some water?" I asked.

"No thanks, ma'am. I'm fine," he said. After more than
five minutes went by, he still hadn't moved a muscle. He was
like a block of stone, with the lavender-scented pillow still
covering his eyes.

All of a sudden, Bob began to cry out, "We need some
protection here!" He lifted his arm and pointed. "Go over
there and protect those guys!" I knew I had to follow what he
asked me to do, so I raced over to the window at the northwest corner of my office where he had indicated and held
up my palms. In front of the window stood two spirits. I
could see the fire escape and the buildings across Broadway
through their bodies, and I knew the men standing there
were the friends from Bob's bracelet.

With my palms up, I sent Reiki to the two spirits while
I whispered to Gabriel and to the guardian angels of the
men standing before me, "Please! Help! Gabriel, dear angels,
please help these spirits!" In a split second, the men were
surrounded by golden-white light. I felt the men responding
quickly to the powerful love that washed over and through
them, and I watched as they surrendered their anguish, transforming into light in the presence of the angels who had
come to bring them home.

Just before the spirits left with the angels, they gave me a
message for Bob. "Tell Bob we are grateful to have had him

for a friend and as our commanding officer during our time together. Please let him know that we are safe." I watched the golden-white light around them grow brighter and brighter. Just before they disappeared, the light intensified in one final surge, absorbing them completely, and then in a flash, the light was gone. The Marines had gone home.

Another ten minutes of complete silence passed before Bob finally stirred on the table. Once he was fully awake, I helped him to sit up and I explained what had happened. He was stunned. "I pointed, and I spoke out loud?" "Yes." He had no recollection of any of it. With emotion, he queried, "My friends were in front of the fire escape?" "Yes." "The *fire escape*?" he asked again. I saw his eyes fill up with tears before he bowed his head so I wouldn't see, and I understood the significance that escaping fire held for him. When I conveyed the messages from his friends, he looked up at me and nodded to let me know he understood.

∞

There are so many people out there who have been traumatized by war and by other things as well. Once PTSD takes hold, it can tear families apart, because it is passed on to others. There is even a name for it, "secondhand trauma." The fact is, anyone can ask the angels for help, not just me on their behalf in a Reiki session. All *you* ever have to do is call on angels for assistance. They are there for anyone who asks. Angelic healing is something more powerful than words can ever say and is something that you can do for yourself, just by

asking. The angels can help wit
say "thank you" as part of your [

Ceremony:
Angels Breaking Unhea

This is a ceremony for anyone v
of disconnecting ties to trauma
would like to disconnect from a:
this ceremony.

Disclaimer: This ceremony
medical therapies. It is an integra
in conjunction with medical trea

Have a piece of paper, a pe
Keep in mind that you will be
have everything arranged so yo
ceremony is over.

Light a candle and call your
with the Archangels Ariel, Rapl
with their loving energy surrou
to move on to the next step.

When you feel ready to mc
angels, write on the piece of p;
rience surrounding what you
write as much about it as you c;
what happened come out of yc

When you are done writing
over it, asking the angels for he
extremely emotional—things

resid
don't
A
the ti
and a
free a
Take
the a
them
gone
As
ten st
ing fro
own t
W
ian an
you. Y
for yo

Chapter 5

Angels Helping with Cancer and Surgery

For several years, I have been working with Dr. Sheldon M. Feldman, chief of breast surgery at New York-Presbyterian/ Columbia University Medical Center. We give his patients the opportunity to receive Reiki before, during, and after their cancer surgeries. Dr. Feldman and I have made many break-throughs together in the quest to bring healing to his patients with breast cancer.

Gabriel has always been present as I've done my work with cancer patients. He is my constant guardian, Reiki master in spirit, and treasured ally. Since the angels are connected to each other at all times, it didn't shock me when Gabriel told me that the Archangel Michael always works with Dr. Feldman, helping him to remove cancer cells. I believe this is why Dr. Feldman and I were brought together in the first place. My heart tells me that Archangels Michael and Gabriel made sure that Dr. Feldman and I met!

The times that Gabriel and the angels have helped me in my Reiki work with breast cancer patients could fill a book. Since I work with angels so closely, I can easily say that giving help to patients is something the angels love to do, no matter how things seem to be going. Angels are always present to assist in medical treatments for anyone who asks—whether it is a patient or a caregiver.

Surgery is terrifying. You must lay your body down on a table in a room filled with equipment and instruments that will soon be used to cut into your body. Strangers all wearing masks, covered from head to toe in operating room garb are in charge, and you can already see how busy they are from the moment of your arrival, so you wonder if anyone has the time to understand how you feel. And the plain fact is, every person in that operating room has an all-consuming task to perform in order to ensure a successful surgery, so there really is no one there to take care of the *patient* during the operation.

Having a Reiki master go to surgery with you changes the whole experience. You know there is someone present in the room who knows you, understands you, will channel the healing love of Reiki into you, will hold on to your life during the procedure, and will be there to welcome you back when you wake up. This creates a much different experience in which you know you are supported by the energy medicine of Reiki and nurtured as a whole living being. In this kind of healing environment, doctors get to do their very best work.

Clinical proof is mounting that shows how beneficial it is to combine allopathic medicine with Reiki. One thing for sure is that patients themselves are proving that they feel so much better going through the allopathic treatments when they receive Reiki as part of their protocol. What follows are two additional stories about powerful experiences I've had while assisting breast cancer patients.

Lynn's Surgery

As mentioned, every time I begin a session, I do an opening prayer to call in Gabriel and the guardian angel of my client, which in some cases brings tears of joy and relief to the person I'm working on. For example, a woman named Lynn, a stunning redhead, arrived at my office for a pre-surgery Reiki session. She had just been diagnosed with breast cancer two weeks before, and surgery had already been scheduled to remove the tumor and to assess whether or not she needed chemotherapy.

As the session got under way, the Archangel Michael appeared to let me know he was working on her healing. When I mentioned that he had announced his presence, Lynn burst into tears. "I've always asked for Archangel Michael to help me, ever since I was a little girl. I'm so glad he's here with me now. I'm just so happy that he's heard my prayers and that he's lending me his healing powers now, when I need him the most!" When her sobs subsided after a few moments, she fell into a deep, healing sleep as the angel-infused Reiki poured into her.

On the day of Lynn's surgery, it was late autumn. The trees that line West 168th Street were ablaze with red and golden leaves, the sight of which filled my heart with joy as I walked down to the Milstein Building after leaving the subway station. I met Lynn and her sister, Diane, in the lobby. As she introduced us, Lynn told Diane that the Archangel Michael had participated in the Reiki session we'd had together the week before. Her sister sighed with relief, since she too had strong connections to Michael.

I'm always learning new things about the possibilities that exist and am repeatedly being encouraged by the angels to expand the ways in which they can help me with my work. The fact that Lynn and her sister had such a strong connection to Archangel Michael inspired me to try using the angels' help in a new way. This was the first time I consciously asked Gabriel and Michael to help during the nuclear medicine procedure, which is the administration of a shot of nuclear material that travels through the body.

To explain further, lymph nodes close to the site where a tumor exists are normally examined to see if they contain cancer. In the case of breast cancer, the sentinel lymph node, or the first node to which cancer may have drained, is under the arm. By the time surgery is under way, the nuclear material from the shot has traveled to the sentinel lymph node and Dr. Feldman locates it with a Geiger counter. He then removes it and it is sent to pathology to determine whether or not the cancer has spread from the tumor into the node. The answer to that question determines if and what treatment may be necessary following surgery.

As Lynn lay down on the upper part of the table, the technician explained what was going to happen and prepped Lynn for the injection that would be made directly into her breast. Then the nuclear medicine doctor arrived. I silently called to the Archangels Michael and Gabriel for assistance and felt their love flood through me and into Lynn's hand, which I was holding while the doctor was administering the shot. I've been present at times when it was painful for the patient to receive that shot, but with the help of the angels, Lynn's was quick and easy, and she felt no pain at all. Then the part of the table she was lying on began to move forward into a tube, where the nuclear medicine could be seen on a screen to show that the injection had been a success.

Afterward, we walked back to the pre-op area, where technicians and doctors who were part of the surgery team came in to introduce themselves. I continued to give Lynn Reiki through her hand, sometimes through her shoulder, and I felt the presence of Gabriel and Michael as a constant. With angelic love flooding all the space around us, Lynn was very relaxed and even sleepy before Dr. Feldman came in for a brief chat and to mark the breast that was to be removed. I could feel the angels helping induce calm as we waited to go in for surgery.

Soon, the anesthesiologist came to walk us to the operating room. As Lynn was helped onto the surgery table by the kind and compassionate OR nurses, I took a moment to silently thank Archangels Gabriel and Michael for being present. Once the whole team was assembled and Lynn's surgery got under way, I silently called in the guardian angels of all the other doctors, nurses, and technicians who were in the operating room. The room instantly filled up with peace and feelings of joy.

This calling in of everyone's angel was another new thing implemented that day. I wondered to myself, *Why didn't I ever think of these things before?*

What transpired was the most amazing surgery I had ever been part of up until then. The energy in the room was wonderful, supportive, and full of angelic love. There was a noticeable ease to everything, and I'd never witnessed a surgery that went more smoothly.

Lynn's sentinel node was removed and sent to pathology. I prayed for a good result. A short time later, the phone in the OR was ringing to deliver the node test results from pathology. The whole room cheered with happiness for Lynn when Dr. Feldman relayed that pathology had found her sentinel node was clear, which meant that the cancer had not spread!

The plastic surgery team came in. At the end of their work, a new technology was introduced. The procedure involved the infusion of a special dye administered by the anesthesiologist. After a few seconds, the lights in the operating room were turned off and what we saw on a newly invented screen overhead was a live picture of Lynn's tissues and veins beautifully reconnecting themselves. The screen demonstrated that the blood flow to the skin of her newly created breast was robust. I gasped to see it—it looked like heaven, like something out of an episode of *How the Universe Works*.

But what we were seeing were streaks of white light as the newly sewn skin and veins knitted themselves back together, right before our very eyes. It was wondrous beyond words.

Since Lynn's surgery, I have made it a practice to call in as many angels as possible to every medical procedure I am part of. She went home from the hospital the very next day. When Lynn called me to say thank you, she was feeling fantastic and looking forward to living in perfect health once again.

That's how it often goes—I meet a client sent by the doctor. We either have a Reiki session or two in my office or I meet the client on the day of their surgery. We go into the operating room, the patient goes home feeling fine, and that's usually the end of my part of their story. Yet I know that once a person has cancer, they live with the possibility that it may come back at any time. I think it's significant to note here that much progress has been made in the treatment of cancer. New medicines and procedures are being implemented all the time, and the angels really can get us through anything, no matter what we may have to face in our future. The next story proves just that.

Angels in Action
During Sue's Breast Cancer

I'd now like to share a case where I was with the client throughout the course of more than a year. Dr. Feldman sent Sue to me after her diagnosis of stage four triple-negative breast cancer. She had already been told the cancer was very advanced, that this form of cancer could be very aggressive, and that it didn't always respond to treatment.

When Sue showed up at my office for her first appointment, I was really worried from the minute she walked through my door. Up until then, even young mothers with little children had come to me for Reiki, and they were certainly very upset to have cancer. Yet in all the time I'd been working with breast cancer patients, Sue was the most distraught woman I had ever seen. She was in a complete daze, practically staggering as she made her way to my office sofa so we could talk a bit before her session. I wondered if she was in deep shock or if perhaps she was on heavy medication.

Sue was feeling a lot of personal guilt about her situation because she had delayed having a mammogram when the lump in her breast first appeared, on the advice of someone who wasn't a doctor. As I observed her emotional and mental distress, I silently prayed to Gabriel and the angels for their assistance. When Sue finally got on my table, I covered her with extra blankets to hopefully stop her nervous shivering. I opened our session by calling out loud to the angels, asking them to help.

Usually a woman with breast cancer cries the first time I see her, which is an important part of the healing process. Releasing through tears creates an energetic shift within the person. Tears clear out some of the terror, which makes room for something different to take its place, including the unconditional love of the angels in the Reiki that supports healing. But Sue's first session was devoid of tears. I interpreted this to mean she really was in shock.

By the time Sue left my office, she appeared to be in a more relaxed state, but I was still worried. It didn't surprise me at all when she called me the next day, crying hysterically. The shock had worn off and reality was beginning to set in.

Sue wanted me to give her Reiki in her apartment, since she felt too upset to leave her home. Fortunately, my schedule for that day enabled me to go to her.

When I arrived at her apartment, Sue met me at the door with a look of terror on her face. I knew she needed to talk to Dr. Feldman—he has a way of calming his patients by compassionately presenting encouragement from a medical point of view. So before we even began the Reiki session, at my suggestion, Sue left Dr. Feldman a message. I knew from past experience that he would call her back soon.

As she lay down on her richly decorated bed, Sue's words tore at my heart. "Maybe I should give Lucy (her dog) away. I'm afraid I'm going to die." I told her, "Don't give Lucy away so quickly. Let's see how things go before you make any hasty decisions."

The Reiki session got underway with Sue resting comfortably. As I opened the session, Gabriel and Sue's guardian angel entered the room. With little furry Lucy resting on the bed at Sue's feet, we all shared a powerful Reiki session together. Dogs always know when something is wrong with their owners, and the angels soothed not just Sue, but Lucy, too. By the time I was done, Sue's stability was more pronounced.

"Thank you, Raven," she said. "I do feel better now. I just want to live." I felt a heightened sense of peace as the angels responded to what she had just said.

Sue called me the next day to say that Dr. Feldman had phoned her back right after I left. Between his compassionate words and the angel-filled Reiki, she was feeling quite a bit better.

Within the week, Dr. Feldman suggested Sue ask me to attend her chemotherapy sessions. Sue had already read that I do not attend chemotherapy with clients because I myself got sick from doing so in the past.

"Raven doesn't do that," Sue told Dr. Feldman.

"Just ask her," he encouraged.

Since the request had come from Dr. Feldman himself, I decided to give it one more try. So in April 2012, I went into the infusion center with Sue, this time wearing a pair of rubber gloves from one of the boxes in the chemotherapy suite. Since I had no adverse effects from giving her Reiki with rubber gloves on, I decided I would accompany Sue to her chemotherapy treatments every week.

The prescribed regimen was to be an eight-month period during which Sue would be having chemotherapy three Thursdays in a row with a week off, and then back on for another three weeks. On her off weeks, Sue came to see me in my office for her Reiki sessions, which felt like going on vacation to the both of us, since it's so peaceful there and she didn't need to be hooked up to bottles of chemicals.

A very distressing part of having cancer is the feeling of losing control over your life. Appointments with doctors, who decide how you will be treated and when, become your central events. Nurses connected to the doctors follow through on the doctors' orders, scheduling tests and procedures that are often terrifying. The only thing you seem to be in charge of is to somehow work up the courage to go through what everyone else is deciding for you. Having a

Reiki master and the help of the angels can assist anyone facing the medical trials that go on for months, and in some cases, for more than a year.

When someone is getting chemotherapy for breast cancer at New York-Presbyterian/Columbia University Medical Center, part of their protocol is to have frequent visits with their oncologist. During those visits, the patient's blood is tested to see if he or she can continue to withstand the upcoming chemo sessions or if they have to wait until their blood count improves before more chemotherapy is administered. At one of those appointments in the earliest stages of treatment, Sue's oncologist told her she would have to have chemotherapy treatments for the rest of her life. The other news was that there was no point in her having the breast surgery, because one of her tests revealed that the cancer had spread to her lungs.

The appointment at which this news was delivered had come right before Sue's scheduled chemotherapy infusion. She cried in anguish during the hours of her chemotherapy. I silently called to the angels from the depths of my heart while alternating between holding Sue's hand and administering Reiki through the bottoms of her feet or sometimes through the top of her head. I was more determined than ever to let the angels do their part and to keep my ego in deep check, preventing it from riding on the bandwagon of fear, so I could deliver my best work.

Sue and I fought for her life as we bonded our hearts together with love. We jumped into the river of her Reiki-infused allopathic treatments and held on to each other for all we were worth. We decided Sue could withstand everything, so long as we stuck together—together with each other, and with the angels. Sue's Rabbi had given her daily prayers to say, one of which included the lines, "May the angel Michael be at my right and the angel Gabriel be at my left; and in front of me the angel Ariel, and behind me the angel Raphael." Through Sue's own prayers, angels were intensified as part of her healing team. I could feel the luminous presence of Gabriel in particular all around us as a constant source of loving power. It was a comfort for me to feel his love as I silently conversed with him, asking if he could somehow reverse all the negative predictions.

I don't know how to describe the kind of relationship that develops between two people when they are facing life and death together. As I gave Reiki to Sue hour after hour through those months, we learned more about each other than maybe anyone else will ever know. We forged an unbreakable bond of trust as our love for each other grew, until we felt like we were sisters. There were even times when we would laugh together like little girls during her infusions as we shared some of the hilarious stories from our childhoods.

After about three months, the nurses in the infusion center told Sue she would have to have a chemotherapy port put in because the chemicals had collapsed her veins and they were having problems giving her the medicine. A chemotherapy port is a little device inserted into a vein just under the skin of the chest. The port provides easy access to the bloodstream for the infusion of the chemotherapy drugs.

Once more we had an entire session in which Sue couldn't stop her tears. The reality of having to endure chemotherapy for a long time to come now registered within her as an unwanted truth. She was already facing a scan to determine if the first months of chemotherapy had created any positive changes, and now she would also be having surgery to insert the port.

Understandably, she was frightened and felt more vulnerable than ever before. In those moments when Sue was feeling such hopelessness, Gabriel had me tell her she could look at this in a more positive light. Now she wouldn't have to face needles each week. He also said that Sue should wait and see what the scan revealed before falling into despair.

"We are working very hard," Gabriel whispered to me.

The port insertion surgery was scheduled to take place after Sue had her scan. On the day of the insertion, she and I traveled together by taxi to New York-Presbyterian Hospital, where Dr. Feldman was going to perform what would be a quick surgery.

From the moment we met up early that morning, Sue was shaking. We held hands in the taxi as it flew up the Henry Hudson Parkway. While aligning myself with the energy of Gabriel, I took time to breathe in the sparkling air of the sun-kissed Hudson River on our left and all of the newly green beauty of springtime in Riverside Park on our right. It took hardly any time at all to reach the hospital. Before we knew it, we were in pre-op with Sue in her blue gown, booties, and head covering, and me in my scrubs.

Dr. Feldman came in to say good morning like he always does before surgery. His kindness and calm demeanor always bring comfort to his patients. This time, Dr. Feldman came through the opening in the curtain surrounding Sue's bed, beaming a happy smile.

"Sue, your scan results are fantastic! The chemotherapy is working very well!" And then came the shocker. "You started out with fifty lesions in your lungs, and now almost all of them are gone!"

This was the first time we'd heard that Sue had so many—*fifty!* Her eyes were wide as Dr. Feldman went on, "The lesions that remain are very tiny and dull, and the tumor in your breast is much smaller. Things are going great for you!"

The surgery went smoothly, and after the port was put in, Dr. Feldman came to see Sue in the post-op area. As he sat by her, I was holding her hand and giving her Reiki on the other side of the hospital bed.

"Sue, I can't tell you how happy I am at your progress," he enthused. "This means you will be able to get the breast surgery after all. I foresee the surgery taking place around February." My heart skipped a beat as Sue's face lit up with pure joy.

Things began to change drastically, and Sue's oncologist began to adjust her prediction about chemotherapy. Rather than face the infusion center for the rest of her life, Sue was being told she would be able to have oral chemotherapy. This was huge!

I'll never forget Sue's final day in the infusion center. When the bell went off to indicate that the last bottle of chemo was done, we both screamed and hugged each other! We were leaving and never coming back, and the ride home in the car from the hospital that day was one in which Sue and I overflowed with relief and happiness.

As things turned out, Sue didn't have to wait until February 2013 after all. Two months ahead of schedule, on December 13, 2012, Sue and I were in the operating room waiting for Dr. Feldman. She was about to receive the breast cancer surgery she was initially told she would never get. She had already been anesthetized and was unconscious when Dr. Feldman entered the OR, holding his scrubbed hands up to be gloved by the nurse.

I said to him, "Dr. Feldman, I promised Sue we would call the archangels here for her surgery. Would that be okay with you? Or do you want me to do it silently?"

"Anything for the patient!" he replied, as was his motto. He began calling everyone together as he was helped into his blue surgery coat. "Okay, everyone, let's all stand around the table." The doctors, nurses, and technicians stopped their immediate chores and took a place around the operating table, with Dr. Feldman coming to stand on my left.

Everyone bowed his or her head while my voice softly called out with a summoning prayer, "We invite into this operating room the beautiful Archangels Ariel, Raphael, Michael, and Gabriel. I ask for the presence of our own personal angels and ask that they help us do our best work here today in service to Sue, and we ask that Sue be restored to perfect health." Then we all stood in silence for another brief moment before

Dr. Feldman lifted his head and moved the team on to proceed with their work.

The operating room burst into a flurry of activity, as the business of surgery got under way. The mastectomy to remove Sue's breast went by without any surprises, and the plastic surgery team inserted the expander to begin the replacement of her breast with ease. Things went easily and everyone commented on how smoothly everything went. But the best was yet to come.

From the beginning of her treatment, Sue had been told that the survival rate for stage four triple-negative breast cancer was only 2 percent. When the tumor board analyzed the pathology of her tumor after it was removed, they made a remarkable discovery. I'll never forget when Sue came to my office to tell me the news. "They can't explain it, Raven, but the cancer somehow *switched* itself from the most aggressive form to the one most treatable."

Then Gabriel whispered to me, "I told you we were working very hard."

In terms of Sue's future treatment, this meant she would no longer need the oral chemotherapy that she was expecting. Instead, the preventive would be taking just one hormone suppressant pill daily.

During her combined treatments of allopathic medicine and angel-infused Reiki, Sue had already experienced a complete turnaround in her fight for her life. There was one more test that had to be done following surgery: another scan that would give the doctors insight into what might need to be done about any remaining cancer in Sue's body. She was very frightened about having the scan, especially in regard to the tumors she feared were still in her lungs. I asked her to please come to me as soon as she got word about the results from her oncologist.

The beautiful picture I snapped of Sue's radiant smile as she walked through my office door, having just been told there were no visible signs of cancer in her entire body, is something I will treasure for the rest of my life! I think our screams of utter joy must have been heard all the way down to Forty-Second Street. We were jubilant enough to kick up our heels and dance on Broadway!

Right after that, I left for England to begin writing this book. During that time, my house hostess, Mascha, brought me to Kilve, a village in West Somerset, England, to visit their Jurassic Coast. As I was walking along the beach, teetering on the endless expanse of rocks, looking for fossils, Gabriel said, "Look down." Nestled in between all the other stones, I saw a small reddish one shaped like a pointed tooth. "That stone is for Sue," said Gabriel. I asked Gabriel why Sue was to receive it. "A mountain was turned into a molehill through the power of love. This is for Sue to keep so she can always remember her blessings."

I picked up the rock and held it to my chest as I whispered "thank you" to Gabriel and to all those who had helped Sue back to perfect health. As I whispered my thanks, I faced the west, looking out over the water toward Wales. Wales, land of the Red Dragon, a conquering power of sacred energy; west, the direction of the Archangel Michael, who guides

Dr. Feldman's hands during surgery. I bowed my head in reverence for this gift that was given and put the stone in my pocket.

When I got back to New York City on June 13, 2013, I gave that stone and a crown of flowers to Sue. This is when her last surgery took place. I had returned from England just two days before, so we hadn't seen each other in more than six weeks. I met Sue at her apartment building at 6:00 a.m. so we could travel together via taxi one last time up the Henry Hudson Parkway to New York-Presbyterian Hospital/Columbia University Medical Center.

When the elevator doors opened in the lobby of Sue's building and she stepped out, we threw ourselves into each other's arms, bubbling over with excitement and laughter. This was it! We weren't facing a life-and-death battle together anymore—this time it was about feeling good about herself. The chemotherapy port was to be removed and a final breast implant inserted so Sue could have a sense of physical balance.

I wore my gram's rhinestone earrings as confirmation that we were celebrating "glamor." After all, we were heading into the operating theater of Dr. Christine Rohde, one of the top plastic surgeons in the nation.

The surgery went very smoothly from start to finish. It was completed in less time than had been predicted. When the surgery was well under way, Gabriel whispered to me, "Keep your right hand across the top of Sue's head and turn your left palm up on your lap." As soon as I did, Gabriel put his hand on top of my mine and filled me up with his divine energy. Gabriel's love poured into the top of Sue's head, ran through her whole body, and moved up into the hands of the doctors. I watched as it filled the doctors and flowed out of them into the operating room. The surgery team had been listening to Pandora and I found it hilarious that as I watched the OR fill up with angelic light "Sweet Child O' Mine" by Guns N' Roses began playing on the radio. Gabriel really does have a sense of humor.

The surgery was over before we knew it. Taking stock before leaving the OR, Dr. Rohde commented, "Gee, that was quick! And boy, does she ever look great!"

Sue recovered from having been under anesthesia at record speed once we arrived in the post-op area. She looked beautiful, even right after surgery; in fact, she was glowing and looked like she had just come back from vacation, not from an operating room. After an easeful afternoon and evening under the careful observation by the hospital staff, Sue was sent home the very next day.

When she came to my office one week later for her weekly Reiki, Sue looked absolutely gorgeous. No one would have ever guessed all she had been through in the past year. She happily expressed to me yet again, "I'm cancer free! It's a miracle!" We had all done our parts to get her there—doctors, nurses, technologists, anesthesiologists, Reiki … and angels.

I know at this point you must be wondering if some of my clients have died or subsequently gotten sick again in spite of all our efforts. Up until now, my clients have always been victorious. But that doesn't mean this will always be the case. Each individual's higher self has his or her own chosen destiny. No matter what may happen to clients after surgery, or following any other allopathic treatment, the angels will always help wherever and whenever they are called upon to do so. You don't need a Reiki master to ask the angels to assist you!

Gabriel tells me I am destined in my future to assist those who have severe trials to go through in order to re-establish their wholeness. It's just a plain fact that there are great spiritual lessons that come in the throes of illness. Yet no matter how difficult the trails induced by disease, a person's higher self is always striving for union with the One Love we call God*dess*, and angels are experts at helping each of us make headway with that! All we ever have to do is ask!

Meditation:
Amplify Allopathic Medical Treatments

Bring your awareness to your breathing. The air brings life to you every time you take a breath. Just with your thoughts, say "thank you" to the air for its life-giving gifts as you breathe normally. Continue saying "thank you" with each inhalation for ten breaths.

Next think to yourself, *I call the golden light of the angels to fill the air all around me.* The angels are always waiting for us to summon them, so the sparkling light comes right away. Let the air fill more and more with golden sparkles, whether you see it, sense it, feel it, or just know that it's happening. Take your time and enjoy yourself.

Without any strain and without putting any pressure on yourself, move your awareness into the center of your chest. Yes, your whole chest rises with each inhalation, yet you seek to focus on a point between your breasts inside your body where you will notice there is a space that is roundish in shape. As you breathe in, notice that roundish place filling up with the golden light sparkles. In no time, after just a few breaths, there are so many sparkles that the space in the center of your chest is full of solid, golden light.

Now as you exhale, send or allow the light from that roundish space out into your body. You breathe in more sparkles, and as you exhale, the healing angelic light travels farther and farther into your body, until it fills every part of you. Be the witness to this and without words, say "thank you."

You can send this light to any and all places that need extra help, if you wish. Whether you do or don't send it to a specific place or places, the light automatically continues to balance, heal, and harmonize your entire body, emotions, spirit, and mind.

Stay with this practice of breathing the light of the angels for as long or as short a time as is comfortable and/or appropriate for you. Then bring your awareness back to where you physically are in the present.

I'm looking forward to a future in which Reiki is used much more abundantly during surgery. Although many hospitals are accepting Reiki as a viable treatment option for patients in tandem with allopathic medicine, to my knowledge, New York-Presbyterian/Columbia University Medical Center is currently the only hospital allowing Reiki in operating rooms during surgery. I look forward to a time when having Reiki during surgery is common practice.

Although Reiki is at the foundation of much of my work, you will see in the coming chapters that my involvement with angels covers a much broader spectrum of the work I do in the world outside of operating rooms, medical situations, and the like.

I saw the angel in the marble
and carved until I set him free.
—MICHELANGELO

CHAPTER 6

Special Angelic Blessings

I'd like to share some very special times in which Gabriel and the angels assisted me spiritually, expanded my awareness, and strengthened my faith.

Angelic Visions Becoming Manifest

While on a vacation in Connecticut in 2012, I was enjoying a warm summer evening of watching fireflies and listening to the frogs calling to each other across the waters of the lake. Joining in the serenade were the peepers and the night insects singing in the trees all around me. Suddenly, Gabriel appeared before me and gently touched between my eyebrows. I began to experience a vision of myself on the Tor, which is a high hill in Glastonbury, England, that is crowned with a tower dedicated to the Archangel Michael. In the vision, I was sitting back-to-back with my shaman friend, Tony Barr.

When the vision was over, I quickly sent an e-mail to Tony, who lives in Canada, telling him what I had just seen. His words back to me were immediate: "How about we make that vision come true on December 21?" which would put us there for the winter solstice and the end of the Mayan calendar.

When I returned to New York City, Gabriel began to speak through me to my meditation students, relaying new information. He continuously affirmed that we were approaching a coming age of light, love, and planetary healing. He spoke to us about Oneness and explained that no matter how different we might think ourselves to be, we all come from the same source. I found it incredible when Gabriel began to introduce us to beings in the faerie realm, explaining that these "allies" were the holders of vast knowledge about nature and natural healing.

"Every being upon the earth who wishes to participate in the global transformation is invited to do their part," said Gabriel. "We give thanks to you for asking for angelic assistance as you move forward in this quest."

Tony Barr came to New York City in October. We wanted to ask for more information as to why Gabriel had sent the vision of our sitting back-to-back on the Tor. While holding the question "why" in our hearts, we listened to shamanic drumming. The drumbeats brought us to our individual spirit guides, who gave us the components of a prayer. The prayer was "A Wish for World Love" and it was to be recited on top of the Tor at midnight on December 21, 2012. Tony was told that people from all over the world would be joining in the recitation of the prayer in matching time zones. Here is the prayer that was given:

To the Gods and Goddesses of many names: We ask for One Life, One Dream, One Love, One Tribe. We ask that seven billion people walk with Love in their hearts for each other, Mother Earth, and all the Unseen Magic. With hearts full of love and gratitude, Blessings to All!

Once back in Canada, Tony contacted me with news that his spirit guides were telling him a ceremony was needed at Mont Saint-Michel in France to prepare the way for the one we would be holding on the Tor. Tony felt it would be stronger if we did the ceremony in France together. I didn't feel pulled to go, but I decided to ask Gabriel during a meditation if my presence was really needed.

In that meditation, I was taken to the Cavern, a special place in my spiritual geography, where a raven was waiting for me. The raven brought me to the Ancients, who were sitting around a campfire. The raven relayed that the Ancients would help me reach the Land Spirits of Mont Saint-Michel, and that I should ask those spirits if they wanted me to come.

After a moment of gazing into the flames, very old souls beckoned to me through the fire—they told me they wished to feel the Goddess again, that there was only male energy surrounding them and they were missing the feeling of the Divine Mother's love. One of the Ancients from around the campfire then advised me, "Stand up now—no more HIDING! You are destined to carry the Goddess energy to all."

I bowed and shyly asked, "But what if I don't want to go to France?" The raven answered. "Not wanting to go is reason enough not to ... only go if your heart leads you there."

It wasn't until we were already in England that I made my final decision to accompany Tony to France. Although I still didn't feel connected to Mont Saint-Michel, my heart began to stir with compassion for any souls who might wish to feel the love of the Divine Mother. How could I deny whatever part I could play in bringing comfort?

Mont Saint-Michel

On December 17, Tony and I left Glastonbury at 4:00 a.m. for an early morning ferry across the English Channel. The trip in the dark of the early morning was magical! Even before we got into the car, a badger had already crossed our path. Once on the road, owls flew overhead several times, and we even had a deer run alongside our car for a while.

At the ferry terminal, Tony drove the car onto the parking deck and we excitedly made our way up the stairway to take our assigned seats. Our passage was to be made in the very first row of an upper level, directly in front of the huge windows at the bow of the boat. For our crossing, Tony and I alternated between falling asleep in the comfy seats, watching the shores of France come closer, and going out onto a windswept deck to drop crystals into the channel waters once every hour. It was wonderful to be refreshed in the cold, salty air. Tony looked like he had stepped out of another time, with his blond hair blowing in the wind and his long, black coat swirling around him. I thought about the ancient ancestors who had crossed these waters ages before we were ever born and sent blessings to them from my heart.

Mont Saint-Michel is an enormous castle erected in honor of the Archangel Michael, which we could only get to by bus from a parking lot about a mile away. Built on rock that is surrounded by the Atlantic sea, at high tide it appears to rise up out of the water like something from a fairy tale.

The closer we got, the more uncomfortable I felt. I didn't feel welcomed into the energy of Mont Saint-Michel at all. As the spirits had mentioned in my meditation, I felt only male energy. The presence of the divine feminine was totally absent. What lodged in my stomach more than anything else were feelings of terror, death, and loneliness. But why did I feel these things?

We did our ceremony that night in the dark, high up on the side of the castle in a little courtyard where there were some trees and stone benches. In the wind and rain, Tony and I followed our inner voices to create a healing ceremony, calling to the Archangel Michael to bless us with love and to empower all that we did.

The ceremony we performed was strong and otherworldly, so much so that I don't remember it at all, except placing crystals in many spots around the courtyard, including at the base of the trees. Each time before I bestowed my crystal gift, I sent my awareness into the ground, attempting to feel the energies within the earth beneath our feet. I could sense, ever so faintly, a longing to be acknowledged and the desire for love.

As I placed each crystal, I prayed to the Divine Mother, evoking her presence as a blessing to all who had died there long ago so they could feel her love as a healing that would release their sorrow.

It wasn't until months later I discovered what I had tapped into. I came upon an article by Phillip Coppen in which he describes how legend and archaeology indicate that the ancient Celts, who were there long before Christianity, held the belief that the place where Mont Saint-Michel now stands was a gateway for the dead to enter the otherworld. The Celts revered the Goddess and believed they returned to her in the otherworld after death. My feelings suggested it was the ancient Celtic ancestors who were crying out to feel her presence honored there, since patriarchal Christianity had claimed ownership over the land.

I also discovered reports of nuns being burned alive in the 1500s after being judged evil for their psychic gifts. This made so much sense to me; when one is devoted to spirit, gifts arise that historically were not allowed in the strict confines of most religions.

The Winter Solstice

I woke up early on December 21 and picked up my journal. *Gabriel, it's the winter solstice and the end of the Mayan calendar today, and here I am in Glastonbury, just as you showed me in the summertime vision. Do you have anything you wish to say this morning?* I wrote. I received the following reply:

All Is One. When a song is sung upon the earth in a loud voice, the intention behind the words is what matters most.

*Songs are being sung in many languages—songs of peace
and of love. All who raise their voice in prayer and song
come from One Heart. All Hearts. All One.*

I went out into the Chalice Well Gardens to join those who
had come to celebrate. As the Mayan calendar came to an end
at 11:11 a.m., the moment was honored with a group meditation around the Wellhead. Wishes for peace were sent out into
the world with a final Om. Next the Chalice Well Solstice fire
was lit on the lower lawn. Gabriel held my hand as I ignited
the wick of my white taper candle from its flames. My candle
became a torch of love for my students and clients back in New
York City, to be shared by passing the flame from my candle to
theirs.

At 11:15 p.m., a small crowd met out in the Chalice Well
parking lot to make the ascent up the Tor. It was rainy, windy,
and really cold. Tony and I led the way up, excited to be taking the final steps to the long-awaited midnight ceremony.

As we approached the tower dedicated to the Archangel
Michael at the very top, we could hear voices singing, filling
the tower with song. Tony went in to join them straight away,
but I hung back. I felt the need to honor the Goddess by calling to her in the seven directions, and I asked her to tie all the
energy bands together from Mont Saint-Michel to those we
were weaving on the Tor. Gabriel stood as a spiritual guardian while I did my private ritual. When I felt all the connections come together, Gabriel and I entered the tower.

Linking arms with those already gathered inside, we all
began to harmonize our voices by toning, filling the night

with beautiful sounds. As midnight approached, the energy inside the tower heightened to an exalted state. At exactly midnight, we recited "A Wish for World Love" with great emotion. I could feel a host of angels swirling around inside the tower, holding all of us in divine Oneness, including the faeries, who had come to add their love to the ceremony. The wind was blowing through the vacant windows and doors, laden with the power of "A Wish for World Love," coming to join us from the groups who were reciting it around the world. I was happy beyond words to feel the love that my darling son, John, and his beloved fiancée, Dina Joy, were transmitting from their ceremony in Central Park.

Just like the angels had said all along, "A Wish for World Love" had become a global and interdimensional event. Groups in Toronto, Canada; Rochester, New York; Santa Fe, New Mexico; Denver, Colorado; Lisbon, Portugal; Brussels, Belgium; Tokyo, Japan; and even on the high seas had all participated.

A digital photograph was taken in the tower when the ceremony was over. There are translucent orbs in the photo, and there is a large one over my head that is not translucent at all—it looks like a small moon. As the photo was shared right after it was taken, everyone exclaimed, "Look at that! It must be the Archangel Michael!" Whatever it was, I could feel the joy of the angels all around us.

Angels Arrange a Perfect Meeting

I have another tale of being brought together with someone I needed to meet while I was on my writing retreat in Glastonbury. This is just one example of the many mystical ways the angels can lend their aid, if we will ask for their help.

After struggling for hours with the flow of a particular chapter for this book, I asked Gabriel to please infuse me with the inspiration to write. I felt stressed and unhappy about not feeling a real direction for the chapter. "Take a break now, Child. Go up on the Tor and enjoy the sunshine," was the advice Gabriel gave.

It was a beautiful morning, and I was in bliss as I walked up Well House Lane. All the trees and the Queen Anne's lace swaying in the gentle breeze along either side of the road seemed to be waving to me as I passed by. I stopped to admire green fields washed in sunshine and full of sheep grazing lazily in the sun.

Making my way up the hill to the eventual gate that led to my favorite path, I stepped through into fields filled with buttercups for as far as the eye could see. I could feel Gabriel walking with me as I enjoyed the warmth in the air. The peace in my heart was pure joy to experience.

As I made my way up the path, moving slowly along the narrow trail, I bent down to walk under low branches full of blossoms and stopped to pay homage to such beauty. Then moving farther along the narrow path toward where I could see my intended meditation spot, I looked up to see two people already there, engrossed in what appeared to be an intense conversation. Not wanting to disturb them, I sat down in the green grass along the pathway, surrounded by tiny blue and white wildflowers. The trees down below were washed in golden light as I began to open my heart to any messages Gabriel might send.

"Gabriel, I am here to ask for your help to finish the chapter I'm working on. Thank you in advance for any help."

I took out my drum and beat a soft rhythm, feeling Gabriel filling me with love from the place where he stood behind me. I felt so peaceful and happy to be sitting in the sunshine while ravens flew overhead. Before I knew it, some of the wondrous birds landed close to me, cocking their heads from side to side, with feathers glistening in the sunlight. The ravens seemed to be enjoying themselves just as much as I was, as they watched me with their bright eyes. I wondered if they were attracted to me because of the presence of Gabriel.

After a little while, the two people who had been occupying my intended meditation spot parted ways. The man began walking down the pathway toward me. After bidding each other a good morning, he and I struck up a conversation.

He told me his name was Michelangelo Raiano and that he was an author living in Glastonbury. I had the distinct feeling he was being angel-led in what he was saying to me, because he quickly began to describe his rescue from an unhappy life by the Archangel Michael. His eyes were luminous as he told me, "The course of everything I was doing changed once I connected with Archangel Michael, and I never looked back." The change had resulted in his new book that had just been published called *The Answer Is in You*!

I was surprised and delighted. "Gabriel," I silently rejoiced, "how perfect! You managed to send me an *author* as inspiration, and one with a book title in the form of a message!"

It may seem like a small thing, but the meetings angels can arrange are the types of little miracles that build faith and bring us farther along our path. Because of my meeting with Raiano, I was able to go back to my chapter, find the answers to its flow within myself, and experience gratitude for the help that had been sent so quickly and with such perfection in response to my request for aid.

Angels Affirming the Continuity of Life

On the fourth anniversary of my mother's death, I woke up with prayers for her already on my lips. I was praying for my mother to be happy wherever she was, and I asked that she be forever in the presence of angels. My heart was longing for some type of communication with her, and I asked Gabriel if I might have some sort of sign that my mom was still with me, if at all possible.

Right after morning coffee, Mascha drove me to Kilve (the rocky Jurassic beach where Gabriel guided me to Sue's stone). The weather was beautiful, and I felt so graced to be able to have the time to commune with Gabriel while gazing over the stretch of water separating England from Wales.

Mascha was a ways down the beach when I sat on a large stone to rest. Thinking of my mother, I began to speak to her softly, "Mom, look where I am now! In England, and right across the way, I can see Wales!" I felt my heart swell up with so much love and gratitude for the woman who had given birth to me. "Mom, you always said you wanted us to do all of the things you never got to do, and so I honor you as I sit here, in this special and magical place where you never got to come in your lifetime. I wish you could have seen this with your own eyes. I love you so much, Mom." I started to cry with missing her.

At that very moment, my eyes were drawn to a stone close by, where the image of a heart had formed—I couldn't tell how it got there; it seemed like it was drawn with the whiteness from the salt in the water, or from the sand beneath the rocks. But it was a perfectly shaped heart, and I knew my mom heard me. She was telling me she is not gone, and that she loves me, too.

Angels and Emotional Encouragement

When I was about to return to New York City at the end of my writing retreat, I was very sad to be leaving Glastonbury. While sitting at my desk, I heard a loud cawing outside. I looked up from the keyboard to see a flock of crows flying over the tree right outside the window. Within seconds, another flock flew over the same tree coming from another direction, and then came a third. I felt this had something to do with my flight back to New York.

"Gabriel, am I to understand that I am to unite with my flock back home in the States?" I asked.

"Yes," said Gabriel. "The birds in their exuberance are assuring you that you will be happy when you re-enter your usual life."

A short time later, I was sitting in Mascha and Karyn's garden when Gabriel and a host of angels came to surround me. I was washed in soothing love as Gabriel softly said, "It's time to go back, Child. You have more to do with those who are waiting for you. We are always with you, no matter where you go. We love and cherish you forever and will be with you every step of the way."

These are the kinds of experiences I needed in order to make the changes within myself that were going to be necessary to face up to a challenge that was coming in my future. And these were the kinds of things I needed to know in order to inspire my clients to expect miracles. Yes, *expect* miracles, making them partners with me in an even deeper way during their Reiki sessions. By expecting miracles, they could easily release from within themselves their own innate powers to heal, making the Reiki work even faster no matter what they were facing!

Meditation:
Connect with the Wish for World Love

I believe that if we were to do the following meditation from time to time by ourselves, as well as in groups where possible, the world would change into a much better place a lot quicker.

This meditation has the power to activate angels on our behalf toward the goal of a better life for all on our beautiful earth. The style in which it is written and flows is how I teach my physical meditation classes; i.e., you get to travel backward and forward in time. This is not without precedent! Quantum physics points out that time in the present, past, and future are all running simultaneously. This is based on the fact that scientists have observed past effects of experiments being altered by changes made in the present, and obviously the present affects the future.

You can record the following meditation on any of your devices, or have a friend read it to you. It can be done alone or in a group. If you find it helpful, light some incense or a candle and put on some music that you find soothing, but none of these things are necessary for you to have a wonderful experience of getting in touch with your heart's desires.

Sit quietly with your back straight or lie down. The experiences to come can be things you see, sense, hear, or just know; there is no "best" or "better" way for any of this to happen. There's just the way you are wired and how your inner world operates as the unique being that you are.

Bring your attention to the tip of your nose and notice the air going in and out as you breathe. Say "thank you" to the air, which automatically begins to raise your vibrations. Being grateful is the opposite of being a victim, so say "thank you" to the air for a moment or two. ... You may find other things rising up inside you that you are thankful for, and if you do, follow the experience to where it leads you.

When you feel ready to move on, imagine that your thanks transformed whatever you are sitting or lying on into a wonderful sea of kindness. Let kindness sink into your skin where you are touching the sea and allow it to run throughout your whole body.

Now give up the weight of your body and just float, weightless. Enjoy the freedom of just "being" in this moment of weightless enjoyment while you continue to fill up more and more with kindness. Enjoy the peace in your body, mind, emotions, and spirit. Rest.

Now as you continue to rest, call golden light to surround you, to flood your auric field, the field of energy around you that extends six feet in all directions, including through any surface you are resting on, through walls, floors, furniture— nothing can stop the golden light from filling your aura, because you are a unique vibration throughout all of time and space. You are from the One Love, which is infinitely creating more, and never duplicating anything it makes. So now the piece of God*dess* that you are is held in pure golden light, the light of the angelic realm.

The golden light affixes itself to the molecules of air you are breathing. Ask the angels to adjust your cells to their higher vibration of love as you breathe in the golden light. See, hear, know, and feel inside yourself becoming brighter, lighter, freer, and happier with each breath that you take, as you float in the ball of golden light that is all around you. Mentally project, *I ask my guardian angel and any other angels who would like to take care of me right now to do so while my spirit goes on a little journey. Thank you for taking care of the human parts of me while I am away.*

Now move your attention to watching your body breathe. Take a moment to really have the experience of being an observer of the human body you occupy.

Begin to notice the part of you that is observing is being joined by the Archangel Michael. Since the tower at the top of the Tor is dedicated to him, he has come to be your guide to bring you there. You, the observer, take his hand and begin to fly with him. You fly out of wherever you are, going higher and higher until you leave Earth's atmosphere and enter what appears to be deep space. You and Michael fly through the stars, until now when you come to a fog or mist. This fog or mist is a doorway to the past, where the December 21, 2012, ceremony is about to happen on the Tor right now.

You and Michael come out of the mist, and you find yourself standing right inside the stone tower at the top of the Tor. You are standing with others who are making beautiful sounds. Their voices are instruments that make tunes without words. The energy is building all around you as midnight approaches. This is the beginning of a new age of light, and you are here to welcome it by adding your own love to the power of its arrival.

Golden light begins to form around you and around everyone else simultaneously. Each person with you is in an individual ball of light. At the same time, there is a group light that encases everyone. The light that encases you and your companions extends high into the air above you, far out to the sides, and down deep into the earth beneath your feet. The group light is enormous and full of love and blessings.

The hour has come. You join your voice with all the others as you speak together:

To the Gods and Goddesses of many names: We ask for One Life, One Dream, One Love, One Tribe. We ask that seven billion people walk with Love in their hearts for each other, Mother Earth, and all the Unseen Magic. With hearts full of love and gratitude, Blessings to All!

Feel the joy and power of being part of this wonderful ceremony marking the beginning of the new age you have come into together. An angel appears before you with a long scroll of paper with many signatures on it. This is the list of those who have made "A Wish for World Love," which the angelic realm has heard.

You are handed a pen made out of a white feather, and you sign your name to the scroll. The angel nods to you and whispers in your ear, "Thank you for your wish. We will take care of this. We thank you for activating our help."

There is so much love washing over and through you that you gently shut your eyes to keep the tears from running down your cheeks. Let yourself feel all the love that surrounds you. Take a moment to appreciate everything that has happened and that is happening right now.

As you take a breath, the love all around you turns into a magic carpet, and you feel yourself floating on it. In a flash, you travel right back to where you left your body, and your spirit easily glides back in. Feel your spirit return as you once more notice your breathing. Your body is breathing, and you are inside it. Take a moment to notice you are back, as you let yourself rejoice that you have become part of "A Wish for World Love." You have activated and released the power of the angelic realm to help and to heal the human race.

When you are ready, get up, have a drink of water, and, if you can, have a little snack or a piece of fruit to ground yourself back in the here and now.

You'll meet more angels
on a winding path
than on a straight one.
—TERRI GUILLEMETS

CHAPTER 7

Angels Healing Locations

For some of us it is a stretch to consider that the terra firma under our feet is affected by traumatic events and by what people do to it. However, our ancestors revered our planet as a living being that needed to be cared for.

When it comes to working in partnership with angels, there seems to be no end to the training I receive from Gabriel. I am in a constant state of gratitude, respect, and surprise as I am shown how I can enlist the aid of angels to help me in all the different areas of my healing work. One very powerful way in which to receive help from angels is in the clearing and healing of places that have experienced trauma or been abused. It wasn't until after 9/11 that I learned angels can clear spaces when help is needed to bring peace to locations.

Ground Zero, After 9/11

When I was doing volunteer Reiki in the Port Authority Police Department's trailer, I had just finished the usual twenty-minute session with Hank, a sergeant who was one of my regulars. He unexpectedly asked me to come outside with him. When we got to a place away from the door, he looked at me with serious eyes.

"Raven, I'm sorry I had to bring you out here, but I gotta tell you this in private," he said, lowering his voice. "I don't know who else to talk to about this, and I'm hoping you can help. Some of us are seeing ghosts down on the site." He looked down at his feet, clearly uncomfortable at having to tell me such a thing.

"What do you mean, Hank? What's happened?"

"Well, we're *seeing* them. I don't know how else to say it. And we're hearing things, too. Mary heard somebody calling her name, and she's really upset because she lost her partner." He looked up at me then, his gray eyes questioning. "Isn't there somethin' you can do, Raven? You know about these things, and I figured maybe you could help."

Maybe I could help? What on earth was I supposed to do? How could I ever fix the place where three thousand people had lost their lives?

"Hank," I said after a moment, "let me pray about it. I promise to do my best with this. It's not my specialty, but I'll see what the angels advise."

He thanked me and went back to work. I stood there looking out across Ground Zero with a heart even heavier than usual.

I was looking at a pit of rubble, twisted steel, and broken concrete—a wasteland. After so many months of witnessing horror, I felt just as wasted inside. The days and weeks on end of psychically feeling every emotion that coursed through the torn and battered bodies of the men and women who came to my table left me feeling just as broken as the shattered buildings before me.

I was being torn apart trying to digest all of the pain I could feel in everyone who came to my table. Now I had to try to figure out what to do about one more of the many overwhelming problems, the likes of which I'd never imagined.

The cops were seeing ghosts. This was serious. It was okay for *me* to see them—it was an ability I had that I had freely accepted as part of my work—but this was the last thing *they* needed to be dealing with.

I stood staring out over the site, waiting for an answer. But nothing came to me except tears. Finally, I wiped my eyes on the sleeve of my jacket, turned my face away, and headed home for the night. As I was walking away from the pit, I heard Gabriel's voice speaking softly into my mind, touching my heart with love. *"Don't despair. You are not alone. I am right here with you."*

My heart felt lifted.

The next morning, I sat on the carpet in my living room with my journal in hand. I breathed in incense as I closed my eyes and asked Gabriel what to do. When the answer came, it was, as always, straightforward. *"A healing is needed over the entire area where this has occurred."* Gabriel showed me what to do, and what part he would play. We would be working with the ancestors of the land and with the ancestors of those who had died.

The next afternoon, I knocked on the commanding officer's door and told him that I wanted to pray down at the site.

"Just a minute, Raven. I'll call one of the guys to drive you down."

Before I knew it, I was in a PAPD truck with one of the officers. He drove me to the pit and parked with my side of the truck parallel to the edge. Up close, I could see the pit was teeming with people and machinery—construction workers with hardhats every color of the rainbow swarmed the site; other hardhats identified FDNY, PAPD, NYPD, DMORT, and FBI. Massive yellow claws plucked twisted steel out of the mess, swung those broken beams over to waiting trucks, and dropped them in the truck beds for removal from the site. Buckets were dumping loads of crushed cement into other trucks.

From above, it was as if the workers and machinery were moving together in a strange ballet. The dancers and moving parts seemed to be paying homage to a massive American flag that covered several stories of a nearby building. *We Will Never Forget* had been posted in huge letters hanging directly above our stars and stripes.

I couldn't get out of the truck because the OSHA inspectors were there and I didn't have a hardhat, so I opened the door and slid out a little from inside, standing with one foot on the edge of the pit, the other inside the vehicle. With sixteen acres of so much dizzying movement before me, it felt good to have at least one foot placed securely on the earth.

Gabriel had instructed me to open myself up to channel Reiki and to call for the help of angels. I would be sending a massive amount of Reiki energy flooded with angelic love directly into the pit. I raised my arms up and softly began the opening prayer I'd been given:

"I call to the highest of spiritual beings from the highest of spiritual realms. I ask that you join me now and that you seal this entire site in a circle of light and love." Suddenly, I felt the atmosphere surrounding the whole sixteen acres stop as if everything was listening. It felt like the pit had taken a quick inhalation of breath.

There was a brief energetic pause, and then in a flash I felt something terrifying. In a rush of frantic, desperate energy, multitudes of lost spirits were streaming toward me! They had heard me, and they were in need.

I cried out for Gabriel, and he led me in what to do. I screamed out loud *"NO!"* I was instantly ensconced in a shield of protective light. I could then see the spirits—transparent, aware, rippling and shimmering in the sun—hovering before me, but they couldn't get through the light around me, which Gabriel told me later was the Archangel Michael keeping me safe.

Breathing deeply and forcing myself to be calm, as Gabriel had told me to do, I mentally constructed a pyramid of brilliant light beams over the site, extending sixteen acres in my line of vision, with the tip of the pyramid pointing up into the sky. Next, invoking the names of the Archangels Gabriel, Michael, Raphael, and Ariel, and all of the angels I could think of, I called to the ancestors of all these deceased people. I implored their ancestors and the ancestors of the land to help these souls get through the opening at the top of the pyramid. I asked Gabriel to help them to make the way home safely into the Light, where they belonged and deserved to be.

Suddenly there was a huge swoosh of energy moving upward from everywhere around me—like a tidal wave being sucked up by an enormous vacuum.

I stood transfixed, listening for a time that felt like forever. I could feel that many spirits had gone home, but I knew more remained. I was sad that I hadn't been a complete success and blamed myself for it until I heard Gabriel's voice whisper to me, "Good work, Raven. Thank you. Everything is as it should be."

I climbed back into the truck, feeling reassured.

The story above shares with you the first time I was taught how effective angels can be when they are enlisted to help with the energetic clearing of land and the area around places that have experienced trauma. After this first dramatic cleansing I experienced at Ground Zero, the healing of locations has become an important part of what I do, since I love the earth and everything about this magical and sacred planet.

In order to support this type of work, I am most grateful to Gabriel for leading me to study shamanism years ago now. Shamanism acknowledges the life in all things upon Earth and teaches the old pathways to knowing how deeply connected we are to everything. This ancient knowledge has helped me in my work with healing places.

The White Springs and the Hawthorne Tree in Glastonbury, England

In Glastonbury, I have a very special meditation spot inside the White Spring. I say "inside" because it is actually a water temple nestled in the side of a hill. It was created in what was once a Victorian well house.

Everything about this location is washed in mystery and magic. The White Spring flows out of the Tor, which is sometimes referred to as the Holy Hill of Albion and is thought by many to be the most sacred hill in England. In fact, a replica of the Tor was center stage at the London 2012 Olympics.

The White Spring temple was lovingly created by volunteers out of gratitude for the pure waters of the earth and to honor the Spirit of the White Spring itself. These waters are thought to be blessed by the goddesses and faeries of Avalon, and to be imbued with healing properties. Every day, people come from miles around to fill their water bottles from an ever-flowing spigot.

Entrance to the White Spring is through old wooden doors in the side of the hill. When you pass through this mystical doorway, you step into another world. No matter how sunny the day, the interior of the White Spring is dark. The only illumination comes from candlelight.

In November 2010, I reverently bowed my head as I passed through the wooden doors. With my palms together at my chest, I stopped and listened to the sound of water spilling into the center pool as I waited for my eyes to adjust to the darkness. My emotions came alive in memory of the visit I had made to the White Spring earlier in the year. When I'd visited in May, I was finally able to really grieve for my mother, who had passed away the summer before. Thinking of my mom again as I stepped down the few stairs into the rushing water that runs in little streams along all the stone floors, I felt a moment of exaltation. I wondered what mystical happenings might come my way during this visit.

My face felt cool and damp as I made my way deeper inside the candlelit expanse of the dark, cavelike temple. I opened my senses and began seeking out connection to the things I could see, and to the hidden magic in the stones, the water, and the earth.

I was moving to the left of the entrance doors, trying hopelessly to keep my feet dry. Sliding my feet along the watery walkway in the darkened passage, I stepped in front of the center pool. Intending to move beyond it farther, I felt a strange energy emanating out of the pool's water that stopped me in my tracks. I was startled by it and felt the hairs rise on the back of my neck as I looked up at the candlelight flickering on the surface of the water. But my attention was quickly turned away and back to my shoes, which were now filled with icy water.

Moving on, I soon found my way to just where I wanted to be. Sitting myself down on a rustic bench in front of an altar to the goddess Bridget, I continued to think of my mom. This was the exact spot where I had unexpectedly and spontaneously grieved for her during that earlier trip. In my grief, I had found myself singing a song to my mother, with words that flowed into my heart from the realm of the angels. In those moments of my angel-led song, I felt my mom come to me, right there inside the White Spring, in front of the painting of the goddess Bridget.

I wanted to have this experience of seeing my mother again; it was now November 2, right in the time frame when they say the veils between dimensions are thin, allowing easy connection with the ancestors. *Perfect timing!* I thought. *I'm so glad I'm here right now.* I said a little prayer of thanks to Bridget and closed my eyes.

Try as I might, surrender what I would, I still couldn't feel any connection to the specialness of the White Spring. One of my strongest doorways to "knowing" is through my feelings, and I felt nothing at all. It seemed as if all the doors to the Light Beings were closed. I found this incredible! In my previous visits, the spirit of this place had been openly inviting and full of love. But there was no love now.

"What has happened?" I asked Gabriel, who was right beside me.

"This place needs a clearing," Gabriel whispered to me. "Things need to be cleared."

I had no idea what those things could possibly be, but I said back to him, "Okay, I'll do a clearing ceremony."

"NO! NO! NO! You mustn't do that now. Just leave!"

I was disappointed, but I got up and made my way out of the temple. As I went past the center pool on my way back to the wooden doors to exit, Gabriel shielded me in light as strange sounds coming out of the water in the pool gave me the chills. I quickly made my way back up the steps and ran out onto the street, very unhappy to say the least. Since I was leaving for the States the next day, I didn't get a chance to discuss what had happened with any of my spiritual Glastonbury friends before I left.

In between my trips to Glastonbury, I stay in touch with my wonderful and gifted colleagues and friends via telephone and Skype to get all the local news and to keep my connection to the land I love just as strong as I can. I was bereft when I called one of my most trusted Glastonbury colleagues, Celtic shaman Jeremy White, to hear that two tragedies had occurred of a dark nature. With deep emotion, Jeremy relayed to me that the Holy Thorn, a tree that according to legend had been brought to Glastonbury by the uncle of Jesus, had been vandalized.

"Not only that, Raven," he told me, "but the loving energies inside the White Spring have been contaminated."

"What do you mean?" I asked.

"Well, the Holy Thorn was chopped down during the night, and when Tim and I went to the White Spring the other day, the energy in there was so bad my hair stood on end. I don't want to go there ever again."

"Jeremy, do you think these two incidents are connected to each other?"

"I'm not sure, but negative actions are impacting people, places, and things all around the area."

After talking to Jeremy, I called Tim Raven, who is a Vitki (meaning "Rune Magi"—one who does divining and healing of every kind by using the runes). "Hey, Tim! What's your take on the White Spring? Jeremy says you two had a bad experience there the other day."

"That's right, Raven, the energy in there is all screwed up right now." This was double confirmation of what I had felt myself when I was there. "We couldn't wait to get out of there."

"Wow, Tim. When I was there last month, I got spooked and wanted to do a clearing ceremony, but Gabriel told me not to do it."

"That's because you can't do it alone using anything even close to what you would normally do," he replied. "Let me tell ya what, it's bloody awful in there right now! It's gonna take something more than any one of us can do alone to clear the energy in there!" I felt heartsick at this news.

The story about the Holy Thorn tree was just as upsetting. This tree has always been shrouded in the myths concerning Joseph of Arimathea mixed with more recent tales of those who claim the Holy Thorn is a portal to the otherworld, or spirit world.

Joseph of Arimathea was a man who is mentioned in all four gospels. Some of the stories about him say he was the rich great-uncle of Jesus and that he brought Jesus to Glastonbury as a young boy to study with the druids. The origins of the Holy Thorn tree itself begin with Joseph of Arimathea's return to Glastonbury after the crucifixion. According to legend, when he arrived he was exhausted from his long trip from Jerusalem. When he reached what is now called Wearyall Hill, he could walk no farther. He stuck his walking stick—which had belonged to Jesus—into the ground and went to sleep. By the next morning, the staff had grown into a tree. The tree became a shrine for Christians from across Europe and a place for people of all faiths to pay homage to miracles.

The Holy Thorn tree is not indigenous to England. It's a kind of hawthorn that grows in the Middle East and flowers in both spring and winter. A sprig of flowers from the tree is sent to Her Majesty the Queen for her Christmas dinner table every year.

The Holy Thorn was vandalized during a night in early December 2010. Someone chopped off all its branches, leaving the stark remains of the hacked tree trunk, with branches all around it on the ground. People wept to see it. This was considered a crime and became national news in England. Law enforcement from across the country was called in to find the vandals.

After ending my calls with my friends, I turned inward to find answers as to whether I could do anything from across the ocean to bring healing to these two situations. Sitting with my journal, I asked Gabriel what I should do, if anything. He told me that the roots of the Holy Thorn tree were alive and reminded me that I was going to be back in Glastonbury to colead a "Return to Faery" retreat with Signe Pike (author of *Faery Tale: One Woman's Search for Enchantment in a Modern World*). Gabriel recommended that I give Reiki attunements to all of the retreat participants and then go to the Holy Thorn to administer Reiki as a group to bathe the tree in sacred loving energy.

Since Gabriel had not elaborated with any further advice on the subject of the White Spring, I knew he wanted me to seek guidance elsewhere. It seemed obvious to me that Gabriel, who can only speak with words of love, didn't have the language to address the White Spring situation. So what I did next was a shamanic journey to ask if there was anything I could do to help with the spring's healing.

When I first heard about shamanism many years ago, I felt like I was being called to it. When you work with angels, they always let you know when you are on the right track, because when you think of something that's good for you, your heart fills up with joy. That's exactly what happened when I heard about shamanism.

The angels guided me directly to some of America's foremost shamans. It was from these teachers that I learned the core practice of shamanic journeying, which has become an important and wonderful way in which I receive information that I need from other realms. There are many books available on the subject of shamanism, so I won't describe it further here. It's just helpful to know that journeying is a process through which we can gain information, insight, and healing. Through shamanic journeying, I have received (and continue to receive) guidance directly from helping spirits for myself and for my clients.

During my shamanic journey for the White Spring, my spirit was brought to a sacred fire around which many Light Beings were seated. They were conferring with one another regarding the question I had come with.

I was told, "The powers of the White Spring have been misused. Since your heart is committed to solving this issue, we will tell you what you must do. As you walk toward the White Spring, you must summon the archangels to walk with you. Before crossing the threshold, announce in a powerful voice that you are entering the White Spring with the archangels to bring love and blessings to all. Then you and your companions must sing the names of the archangels for as long as you are there. This is how the negative energies will be cleared." I thanked them all, was thanked for coming, and popped back into my living room in New York City.

I got to Glastonbury ahead of the retreat participants in order to prepare everything for them. Then, the day for the workshop participants to come from points across the globe finally arrived.

That evening during the attunement ceremony, I transferred the energy of Reiki that flowed through me in torrents of power.

The next morning, we woke up to sunshine and birds singing. After breakfast, our newly attuned company of healers began to make our way to the Holy Thorn tree. When we arrived at the entry point, I looked out over Wearyall Hill, which was washed in the morning light, and I could see that sheep were standing very close to the tree. It almost seemed like they were waiting for us. As we made our way across the brilliant green grass toward the Holy Thorn, I felt like we had somehow stepped through a veil into another reality.

The love and healing given to the Holy Thorn tree is something I will remember for the rest of my life. To see these women hold their palms up to give Reiki to the tree is a vivid memory seared into my consciousness. Time seemed to stand still; I have no idea how long we stayed, sending Reiki and praying for the life of the tree to continue so feelings of wonder could be awakened in the hearts of future pilgrims traveling to the site.

Over lunch, I explained that although no one was under obligation to do so, we had been given instructions for a special task—to bring the archangels into the White Spring to do clearing and to restore the water temple to its original energetic beauty. No one but me had ever been inside it before, so my retreat mates had no idea what to expect.

Later that afternoon, those of us who were willing made our way up Well House Lane. Before we entered the White Spring itself, I called the four archangels Ariel, Raphael, Michael, and Gabriel to stand with us. I felt the angels as a wall of light around us so strong that heat came into my body from all sides. It was an angelic shield of protection.

Our quest was to enter the White Spring and sing the names of the archangels, asking from our hearts for the waters to be healed. Before we walked over the threshold, I cried out, "We come with the archangels in love. Archangels, please clear this place and restore its true loving spirit!"

We stepped over the threshold, and I immediately felt a malignant force rear up toward us from the pool deeper inside. My heart skipped a beat in a moment of fear, but there was no time for that. I affirmed in a loud voice, "We come with the archangels to the sacred White Spring! The archangels come to bring healing and love."

I commenced to lead the retreat mates in a song comprised of the names of the archangels. We sang full out as we made our way down the steps. The archangels and many other angels surrounded us in their powerful love. As I watched, their light emanated out from around us, filling the whole of the White Spring temple. "Ariel, Raphael, Michael, and Gabriel," we sang over and over again, flooding the inside of the White Spring with the sound of our voices, releasing as we sang the angelic powers to clear and to heal. A visitor who had brought his drum inside began to play along with our singing. The whole of the White Spring came alive with the sound of our voices and the beat of the drum; iridescent white light flowed outward, around, and through, washing everything clean with divine love.

Were we there for fifteen minutes or for an hour? I have no idea.

When I returned the next day, I carefully made my way down the stairs and began to walk around with all my senses open to perceive any and all energetic realities. The beloved White Spring was sparkling, crystal clear, and once more full of love. The joy in my heart was boundless.

Exercise:
Protection in Sacred Places

Many claim the White Spring is a healing gift from the elven king Gwynn Ap Nudd. Places like this should not have their gifts abused. However, wherever there is true natural power, there is always the temptation for some to use that power for their own purposes. No matter what someone else may have done, you can always protect yourself when visiting any powerful place by calling to your guardian angel and asking to be surrounded with their light before you enter.

It's just a good practice to protect yourself whenever you interact with the energies of a place. If you feel the presence of strange energies that don't feel welcoming to you, then don't enter that place. But if there are no feelings of being denied entrance, you can step through and enjoy the high powers of light in any location by following these simple steps:

As you approach the entrance to a place, call to your angel to activate loving light all around you. Stand at the threshold and introduce yourself and your angel to the guardian of the place. Ask for permission to enter. Then wait for the invitation to pass through.

It's as simple as that—just ask your angel to surround you with their loving light before you enter. Remember that like attracts like, so if you enter a place engulfed in the light of your guardian angel, you will be able to safely connect with the higher forces of love that dwell in that location. Angels always keep us safe by surrounding us with the vibration of their purely divine energy.

Exercise:
Clearing Earth Trauma

There are certainly many places on Earth where trauma has been felt, including hurricanes, earthquakes, and war. In those cases, please re-create the calling in of the archangels as I describe in my ceremony at Ground Zero or our ceremony inside the White Spring. I trust my examples of how you and the angels can clear spaces will be of use to any readers who might have the wish, or need, to bring healing to any location.

Make yourself familiar with the angels
and behold them frequently in spirit;
for without being seen,
they are present with you.
—ST. FRANCIS DE SALES

CHAPTER 8

Angels Healing the Past

After Ground Zero was cleared and the site was officially closed, I received a request from the police to conduct a ceremony for those who had worked at the site. At the advice of Gabriel, I held a ceremony where workers placed something of value into a gourd while calling their hearts back to them.

The gourd that had been center stage in that ceremony attained a kind of fame. Although it had been a private event, somehow people from around the world were finding out about it and things began to arrive in my mailbox. I received memorial cards from the funerals of people who had died on 9/11, a stone from Wales, a shell from a beach in Ireland, and many other items. All of the items had an accompanying note with some rendition of the same request: "Please put this into the gourd."

Time passed. Controversy over what to do and when at Ground Zero continued, and no cement was poured while the disagreements raged. Hank was still stationed there and called me one day to say a ghost had just gotten into his truck when he was driving across the site. Ghosts were showing up in the PAPD family center on the south rim. Once again, he asked if I could do something to help the situation.

I got in touch with a New Jersey shaman named Elaine Egidio. Elaine and I began to work together on a ceremony to help the people who had died, as well as the land itself. The ceremony we created would be performed on Father's Day 2003. I invited healers who had worked at Ground Zero along with some members of the police and fire departments to take part. This was our chance to be together again and to maybe even gain some healing that we might still need for ourselves.

On the evening of the ceremony, everyone who came brought offerings to put into the gourd that was once again center stage on our carefully constructed altar. Elaine anointed everyone, including the police, with White Angelica essential oil for protection before calling in the spirits of the seven directions. I then called in the archangels and the angels of the deceased who were ready to go home, recreating the beams of light in the shape of a pyramid over the site as I had done before.

When the drumming started, things began to happen that seemed otherworldly. A wind rose that shook the American flags along the shrine to the deceased, tossing sand into the air all around us. I could feel spirits spiraling upward into the light beams. The circle of healers, police, and firefighters around us supported each other by holding hands as they stood in the raging winds that had come out of nowhere.

When it was all over, the wind ceased and a silence fell over the entire sixteen acres. None of us could speak. After a time that seemed endless, I realized Hank was standing in front of me. I was stunned when he presented me with a folded American flag that had hung over Ground Zero. I could hardly keep from weeping as he said, "I present you with this flag that hung over the World Trade Center site in thanks for all the healing you brought to me and to all the others who struggled here. You never abandoned us, and for that we will always be grateful."

I took the flag and held it up to my chest. "Oh, Hank, thank you, thank you so much," I said.

With that, he picked up the gourd from the altar, slung his arm through mine, and marched us down the ramp into the pit, where he ceremoniously buried the gourd in a pile of sand waiting to be made into cement. Hank saluted the buried gourd and the ceremony came to an end. Hank dug the gourd out and promised he would put it into the cement of whatever building foundation was poured first.

The biggest shock came when I watched the replay of the footage from that night with the crew who had filmed it. During the time when Hank and I had been walking down the ramp in silence, the digital equipment had recorded voices intoning beautiful sounds and melodies that couldn't be explained. The soundman asked, "What do you suppose that could possibly be?" He was sheepish and seemed embarrassed as he continued, "Do you think it could be … *angels*?"

Gabriel whispered, "Yes!"

Months later, Hank called me with sad news. "Raven, the time has come for me to retire. I have to give the gourd back to you." I went down to Ground Zero to retrieve it. Hank was bereft that he had been unable to place it in the cement of a new building, but because of all the fighting about Ground Zero, no building cement had ever been poured. I brought the gourd home with hopes I would still be able to get it to where it needed to be, one way or another.

The event that marked the official closing of my 9/11 duties took place on September 11, 2004. What led up to it was highly unusual. The city was still fighting over what to build on the site, so the gourd remained in my closet. And then it began to cry out to me.

"Please, let us go. We need to be released." I was having terrible nightmares in which all the people's memorial cards inside the gourd came to life and begged me to let them out of my closet. Once more, I began to pray and to ask Gabriel for a ceremony that would release not just the gourd and all the spirits it contained, but me, as well—once and for all.

What Gabriel asked me to do was really beautiful. As I opened my heart to receive his guidance, he conveyed a lesson to me about the sacredness of water. He spoke to me about how the waters of the Hudson River are connected to the Atlantic Ocean. Gabriel said, "All the oceans merge together in deep sharing. Release the gourd into the Hudson and all the love in the gourd will eventually touch all the continents of Earth."

So on September 11, 2004, I met up with some of the healers I had worked with as volunteers and other friends who wanted to be part of this event, including my son John. Ironworker Adam (who had given me his story for my last book) told me that he just *had* to be the one to bring the gourd for release into the Hudson on his boat.

We all met at Chelsea Piers, which had returned to its former commercial use since having been a triage center for many months following 9/11. Adam had rented a slip at Chelsea Piers just for the day of our ceremony. I felt angels all around the pier and on his boat as we followed the directions Gabriel had given.

First, I took the gourd lovingly out of its blue shroud. Everyone present was given a candle, and we all sealed the top onto the gourd with wax drippings. It looked like it had white frosting dripping down the sides by the time we were done.

Once it was securely sealed, I lovingly carried the gourd onto Adam's boat with Gabriel right behind me. Just seven of us could go aboard because he had only seven life jackets, and there was no way twenty-five people could fit onto such a small vessel. As we slowly slipped away from the dock, everyone left behind threw rose petals into the mighty Hudson. The petals seemed to follow us for a time as we sped away.

Adam stopped the boat directly across from Ground Zero. We floated with the engine off. My son and I put our hands on the gourd and we lovingly sent Reiki into it. I felt Gabriel stirring my heart with the words for the gourd's release.

"May the highest of angelic blessings and the greatest of divine love go with you to your great destiny to bless the earth. We lend to you the beauty from the hearts of all of us here in New York City."

At that very moment, one of the party boats that traverse the Hudson was coming along toward us with music blasting. I clutched the gourd to my chest protectively, not wanting its contents to be offended by such a party atmosphere. Just then, the music stopped and a voice boomed out over the water, "We are opposite Ground Zero. Let us have a moment of silence." I was amazed at our timing. I knew it was the perfect time to let the gourd go, so I gently placed it into the river. We threw rose petals after it, and the petals floated all around it as it bounced on top of the waves.

We watched the gourd for as long as we could see it as it drifted on the tide out toward the Atlantic Ocean. It was a shining moment, and there was even joy as the gourd merrily danced on the waves.

Clearing My Ties to Ground Zero

Although I thought my involvement with 9/11 ended with the releasing of the gourd into the Hudson River, there was still more to come for me personally. I had been injured at Ground Zero, but I didn't know it. I had followed my safety protocol and thought I had done a good job of protecting myself, but the situation was extreme. The plain truth is, no one had ever brought Reiki into the middle of a disaster of such epic proportions before; we had entered new territory regarding what it took to protect one's Self.

In February 2008, I was leading a retreat in Mexico when I got a phone call from my friend Allison, who was also my personal acupuncturist, telling me she had contracted a serious illness. She gave me permission to lead my retreat mates in healing rituals on her behalf.

Right after we did ceremonies for Allison, I got pains in my stomach, but I didn't think anything of it. I attributed the pain to food poisoning of some kind.

In spite of prayers and treatments—both allopathic and alternative—by many doctors and friends, Allison's health continued to deteriorate. It was a shock when she passed away in the hospital just after her twenty-ninth birthday. I was stunned and awash in deep grief at losing such a dear friend who had graced not just my life, but the lives of so many others.

During Allison's memorial service, the pains in my abdomen got much worse. I imagined I had picked up parasites in Mexico. I went to see my doctor, who gave me pills to rid me of any parasites I might have had, but the pills didn't help.

As time went by, the pain increased drastically. I began to have attacks accompanied by violent vomiting that often lasted for more than twenty-four hours. Whenever the pain started, I would have to cancel clients, classes, and anything else I might have scheduled, because I couldn't function during these episodes of such extreme pain and vomiting.

I was sure my doctors would uncover the reason for the attacks. Once I knew what was wrong with me, my plan was to use Western medical remedies along with Reiki to cure myself. However, in spite of more tests than I can even remember the names of, my doctors could not find the source of my pain.

Years went by, and after seeing many doctors I was told there was nothing they could do. The recommendation was to just take painkillers when I felt an attack coming on, go to bed, and wait it out. The painkillers didn't really work, so I added my own remedy of giving myself Reiki to help me sleep through the pain.

I don't know why on earth it took me so long to ask the angels to help me with my own health problem, since I enlist their aid on behalf of everyone else who comes to me (pesky human oversight, or maybe just part of the big plan), but one night I was in absolute desperation, bent over and weeping in excruciating pain. I couldn't stand up and was shaking with weakness after so many hours of violent vomiting. I cried out, "Gabriel, please help me! I ask all the angels to please help me!" But the pain didn't decrease at all, and I didn't re-cover from the attack until many hours later in the usual pat-tern of eventual relief.

I talked to a spiritual colleague of mine and confessed to her that I was shaken and didn't understand why the angels hadn't answered my prayer. "They didn't help me," I lamented. "Nothing happened. The pain didn't subside one bit until hours later when it just went away, like it always eventually does."

"Of course the angels are helping you with this," said my friend kindly, her crystal blue eyes shining. "They just aren't going to put a Band-Aid on something serious, you know." She looked at me frankly as she continued, "What you need to do is get to the bottom of what is truly wrong, and now that you have asked the angels to help you, the real answer is certainly already on its way!"

She was absolutely correct. Within days of that conversation, I began to teach a course for Reiki masters. On the Saturday night of the training, I received an e-mail from my friend who was part of the Disaster Mortuary Operational Response Team (DMORT). I had met Gayle Onnen at the Medical Examiner's Office after 9/11. She had finally located a photo she meant to send me two years prior, but the photo had been misplaced. Suddenly, there it was on my computer screen. The minute I saw it, I began to relive the whole scene from more than ten years before when I had first seen the photo.

I remembered it as if it were yesterday. ... Gayle passing the photo over to me. I saw it was a picture of her standing with a police officer. They were standing with their arms around each other on East Thirtieth Street between the morgue and the refrigeration trucks of 9/11 victims' remains, but there was something else in the picture that upset her—there were cloudy shapes standing at their sides, behind and even in front of them.

"What do you think those are?" she had asked, looking at me with eyes full of fear. Although I was quite sure of what we were looking at, I didn't feel comfortable expressing myself while surrounded by FBI, police, and all sorts of government officials.

"Oh, I don't know," I said. "What do *you* think they are?"

She lowered her voice and whispered to me, "Ghosts. I think they're ghosts. Ghosts from the pile."

"Yes," I murmured, putting an arm around her. "I suppose you're right…"

Shaking my head, I snapped back to the present. In her accompanying e-mail message Gayle said, "I haven't felt right since then. I'm afraid some lost spirits got stuck inside me." When I read that part, my heart caught in my throat with worry for her, and I sent a prayer to the angels that Gayle would find her way back to perfect health. In the next second, however, I began to wonder, "Has something like this happened to me? Is this why I'm sick and the doctors can't find what's wrong with me?"

The next morning, I showed Gayle's photograph to my Reiki class in order to prepare them for the possibilities they might be presented with in their healing work. In the safety and bright sunshine of the beautiful class space, I opened my computer and told the story of the photo to my students.

"This distresses me so much to think of Gayle's being so upset," I confided. "She's such a wonderful person, and she did so much for so many after 9/11. It hurts my heart that she is suffering."

Turning her eyes from the screen to look directly into mine, Reiki student Lisa Wolfson said to me calmly and softly, "Why don't you just e-mail this photo to me, and I'll forward it to my friend, Lisa A. She's a really gifted medium. We all call her Lisa A. because she works with the angels—A for angels, right?" Then she laughed and said, "It's also handy for telling us apart. But seriously, maybe Lisa A. can help."

That night I sent the photo on to my student Lisa and she forwarded it to her friend Lisa A.

Upon seeing the photo, Lisa A., whose proper name is Lisa Vento Abbatiello, sent word that Gayle and I could call her for help whenever we would like. As a medium from the New York area, she knew firsthand the spiritual ramifications of the 9/11 attacks. Lisa A. was passionate about helping Gayle and me since we had been working in the thick of it all. I sent the contact information on to Gayle, and then I picked up the phone myself.

The phone rang briefly and a woman answered. "Hello, is this Lisa A.?" I asked. "Yes it is." "This is Raven Keyes. Thanks so much for offering to talk to me, and..." I was flustered and didn't know how to continue, but Lisa A. helped by excitedly saying, "Oh, I'm so glad you called," and other kind things that I can't remember. I was feeling very emotional to be talking again about the subject of September 11. The only thing I can remember clearly from the beginning of our conversation is the trepidation I felt regarding asking her the question I knew I had to ask.

"There is no easy way for me to ask you this, Lisa, so I'll just get right to the point," I said. "Do I have people who died on September 11 stuck inside me?" There was a pause on the other end of the line.

"Raven, no, you don't have people stuck inside you." I exhaled my relief as Lisa A. went on, "Your female family members on the other side are already here with me. They are telling me that people you did Reiki for after 9/11 felt very grateful to you, and they feel emotionally connected to you." My eyes started welling up with tears as she continued, "Your mother, grandmother, and great-aunties are now saying that people who died made emotional ties to you when you worked on their relatives. They couldn't help it, because they were so happy for the comfort you brought to their loved ones."

She went on, saying, "Some of those who died continue to visit you. Your relatives are telling me all of these emotional ties made to you by people both living and dead are energetic cords that must be disconnected. They are saying that only the angels can help you now. You are being made sick by the draining of your energy through these ties. You have to sever the ties and let these people go. Your relatives are begging you to do this, because they are very worried about your health."

As I sat on the sofa in my living room listening to Lisa's loving voice, she gave me instructions, dictated to her by my mom, gram, and great-aunties. In the last part of our conversation, Lisa conveyed a ceremony with the angels my relatives suggested that would sever the ties that were making me sick.

When I hung up the phone, I was beside myself. I was glad to know I had helped people after 9/11, but I certainly didn't want to be made sick from it! My prayers to Gabriel and to all the angels were a constant during a night of remembering back to all I had witnessed.

I had to wait until the next weekend before I could do the ceremony. My mom, gram, and great-aunties had, through Lisa, told me to write down on a piece of paper the story of whomever it was that upset me the very most during all the time I had been volunteering. My family said that by focusing on the most charged experience, I would create an opening through which all the others would be able to follow for release. Once I was done following all the instructions they had given, I was to burn the paper to release the energy held in the written words.

When I finally knelt before my altar, I began to write about the mother who had broken my heart the most. I was transported back to the family center as I wrote, and I could see her face before me as the story poured out onto the page.

It was the story of a woman from Peru who had lost her son. He had been working at Windows on the World, the famous restaurant at the very top of the North Tower. Her eyes as she cried brokenheartedly on my Reiki table had haunted me in my dreams for all of these years.

As I folded the paper up, I was crying again, praying over what I had written and asking the angels to bless the mother in Peru, to heal her, to help her in every way possible. Then I was keening for all those who had died and for all those living who had lost loved ones, keening and praying for them all, asking the angels to bless them, until all the feelings I had denied myself from feeling in the times I had to be strong were all rising up inside me. I threw myself face down onto the floor where I lay screaming for help. "Gabriel! Help me! Help me, angels! Take it all away! Take it all away! I don't want it anymore! Please help me."

That's when I felt two angels step lightly onto my upper back. I was awash in their wondrous love. In perfect timing with one another, they reached inside my body and grabbed hold of what needed to get out. They were able to do this in what felt like mere seconds, and with the slightest of pressure, they lightly sprang off in a flash of light, moving upward very quickly, carrying with them streams of pain and despair. The ties that had been causing my health to be compromised were broken clean, and I felt my tears shift from anguish to relief and joy. In the next millisecond, my whole body was floating in divine love that I could feel all around me and inside me at the same time.

When I could sit up, I folded the paper, grabbed a lighter, and took them with me out the sliding glass doors at the end of the living room. I picked up an empty metal flowerpot as I walked down the two stairs. I stepped onto the patio and made my way the short distance to the wall at the edge of the lake. I put the paper into the flowerpot and set it on fire. I watched as the paper burned and turned into smoke, asking the angels to take the energy of what I had written and please transform it in whatever way was for the highest good of the mother and for me.

As the smoke curled upward, I closed my eyes. I became aware of Gabriel and Michael, and in a flash, they brought my spirit to a place beneath what looked like a membrane that emanated light.

"The energy from the paper you burned has been brought here," said Gabriel as he and Michael opened up a tiny bit of the membrane so I could look inside. What I saw and felt pouring out of that teeny window was a force of love so powerful I knew I couldn't possibly enter in. I knew that if I did, I would disintegrate and become part of the force itself.

The angels quickly closed the opening they had made, and I burst into tears to realize the enormous power of love that is the source of creation. You can call that source anything you like—God, Goddess, All That Is, Universe…

That's when I was told that humans are not physically wired to withstand being in the presence of that kind of power. But that's what angels were made for, longer ago than we can imagine. Gabriel explained to me that they were created to go through the membrane in order to fill up with love. They then deliver the love to whoever calls upon them, administering the exact amount needed in order to be of help. In other words, angels share the pure love that is creation itself in whatever way is necessary for a person to heal or to transform. They deliver the creative power of the universe itself, and the love they bring can help us in extraordinary ways.

As protection for me, I was only allowed to see through that membrane for one split second, but in that moment I felt my heart open and become imprinted with a wondrous gift. I finally understood in every part of my being that we are all made of that loving source, that all things are wired differently, and that nothing is left out of it. Every one and every thing is part of that divinity.

A few days later, I sat with my journal and asked Gabriel to tell me why my illness had its original start seven whole years after 9/11, at the time when Allison got sick. Gabriel wrote, *Allison, as a healer, was committed to your health. Even though she*

was sick herself, a deeply sacred part of her was still leading you to-
ward your own healing. The stress and anguish you felt in response to
Allison's illness was the trigger that began to bring to light what was
very wrong within your body, mind, emotions, and spirit that needed
to be healed.

I thought that was it—that I would be fine and that the
pain attacks were now over, once and for all, but I started
having minor pain episodes. Since my condition had been so
chronic for so many years, I imagined my body was readjust-
ing itself to not getting sick every thirty days or so, which
was the pattern that had formed over time. For me, it was
wonderful that I wasn't getting violently ill for hours on end!

In early June 2013, I went to the site of the temporary
9/11 memorial at Ground Zero. I really had no desire to return to that location, but I was playing tour guide for Mascha
and Karyn's daughter, Elea, who was visiting from the Netherlands and wished to see it. I have to admit, once the subject
of visiting Ground Zero came up between Elea and me, a
tiny little bit of curiosity began to stir—I wondered if maybe
it would do me good to feel how much things had changed
down there after all the years that had gone by.

Elea and I went to the booth on Vesey Street to pick up
our tickets. I could see the passageway beyond the booth,
peopled not just by visitors, but with several uniformly
dressed men in blue shirts who looked at each person's ticket
and guided everyone along the path that stretched before us.
This was so surreal to me that I started to feel dizzy.

I knew that Ground Zero was now a tourist destination,
but the full impact of what that meant didn't register with

me until the moment when we started to walk along a constructed passageway, down toward the site. The blue-shirted Ground Zero workers chatted with each other as they motioned us along. Emotions started rising up from deep within me. *Wait a minute,* I thought as my mind began to whirl in disbelief and shock at the casualness of it all. *This is where we held the ceremony where the officers got to reclaim their hearts!*

As Elea and I walked along, memories like those continued to flood through me. It was a lonely feeling knowing that not one person anywhere around me shared them. As we went through security, I could see that it was just another day for all the workers. And then a profound understanding entered my consciousness. I knew my memories of this place had frozen me in moments of time that had long passed.

Elea and I went to the South Tower pond and Gabriel stood behind me as I cried, running my hands across the names of the firefighters who had died there. Elea hugged me and said, "Raven, I'm from the Netherlands, and I find this place to be very beautiful. They've done an amazing job here, take comfort in that."

After not having had a really serious pain attack since my ceremony with the angels, my visit to Ground Zero brought on another horrific one within twenty-four hours. I was away on business when I felt it start up and couldn't believe it was happening again! It turned into the most violent attack I'd ever had. I was stunned and weakened by the physical effects and the emotional distress.

When I asked Gabriel what had happened to me, he warned me not to return to Ground Zero. "You've done what you can there. It's for others to handle now. Ask Archangel Michael to help you to release your pain. There is still healing you need to do for yourself, from your own past, once and for all. Don't be afraid, and embrace letting go."

"Gabriel and Michael," I said, "I ask to be free. Free of all the illness and pain that has plagued me for so long. I swear that I am ready to advance to the next step, and I ask for my health to be restored."

When I got back to my office in New York City, I began to set up a ceremony in which I could formally ask Archangel Michael to help me. I picked up a wand of birch wood with crystals on each end that had been given to me by a friend. As I faced east, I raised the wand skyward, closed my eyes, and sent my awareness into the natural energy of Central Park two blocks away.

While facing east, I called to the Archangel Gabriel. I then turned slowly to my right, summoning the archangels of each direction as I called them one by one. With God above and the power of Goddess in the earth under my feet, I stood still. I could feel all those energies pouring into and through me, and gave my heart to all that power.

I cried out, "To all the archangels, I say, I am here! I will do the best I can in the time I have upon the earth, but I can't manage to do it to the best of my ability with the fear of getting sick at any moment." I was in tears. "Please, Archangel

Michael, as the one who lifts things out that do not work, I ask you to help me. I surrender my pain to you. I ask you to take out any and all sufferings and sorrows that affixed themselves to me at any time in my life." The tears were rivers of pain. "Please, Michael, I can't stand to be sick anymore! I need you to help me resolve the issues from the past that are harming my body in the present. Thank you from the bottom of my heart, dearest Michael!"

There was no more to say. I stood in silence and observed my inner stillness, just waiting. And then it came. I felt a powerful energetic shift within my body. My heart filled with gladness, though I still had a ways to go in my journey to release damaging ties to the past.

Sometimes we think we've put something behind us, and if there is a flare-up or a reoccurrence there is the possibility of losing faith. But what I've come to understand through the experience of being ill is that when challenges come, we just have more to learn about how to live, and the angels in their infinite, ever-expanding love have more to teach us, if we will just open to ask for the teachings, and for the blessings they have to offer.

I think this is important for anyone who has been suffering for a long time. Perhaps you can ask yourself if you are renewing your suffering by going to a certain place, continuing to interact with people who are toxic to you, or just failing to let go of the emotions that continuously play themselves out, over and over like a record that is stuck. Archangel Michael is the best medicine in these situations, and frankly, your own heart knows what to say and how to ask him to heal you, if you will just sit down and be honest, or stand up and call to the powers that are there for you.

Ancient knowledge dwells within all of us. And then there's the truth that we are all part of the Oneness, so you can tap into the high knowledge of our ancestors and all the knowledge there is in the entire universe through time and space, simply by asking to do so.

Exercise:
Release the Past

Here is an exercise that can be done once, or as often as is needed, until total release of the past is achieved and clear insight into the possibilities of a wonderful future has been restored.

You can make a recording of this exercise so you can do it while you listen, have a friend read it to you, or read it right from the book. You are going to be connecting with angels who will facilitate healing work that needs to be done. Allow things to happen naturally, without putting pressure on yourself; it is not necessary for you to be in a deeply meditative state in order for this exercise to work.

If you like to have incense and soothing music while you do sacred things, then go ahead and prepare everything you need. You might even get a blanket to cover yourself with so you can feel like a child again, which can be psychologically comforting to have the sensation that you are taking care of the child within you. This exercise can be done either sitting or lying down. If you are sitting, make sure your spine is straight and that your feet are flat on the floor. Whether sitting or lying down, keep your arms by your sides, and resist crossing your ankles.

Begin to notice your breathing. The air is truly sacred, and your higher self knows it. Our ancient ancestors were connected to the natural rhythms of life inherent in nature, and they breathed the same air that you are breathing right now. The ancestors revered the air for its life-giving powers. As you notice your breath, begin to silently thank the air for keeping you alive. As you thank the air, just like the ancestors did, you automatically begin to connect with their knowledge about how to allow healing into your life through spiritual channels.

Enjoy the air as you breathe it in—notice how you feel and how much just breathing in fills you up with the positive energy of life itself, and say "thank you" as you exhale. Continue to breathe this way, enjoying the simple act of breathing in life force on your inhalations, and thanking the air on the exhalations, for as long as you like. (If it helps you to have a direction here, do this for a minute or two, without stressing about how much time has gone by.) When you are ready, move on to the next part.

Now begin to breathe in for five counts, hold your breath for five counts, and exhale for ten counts. This five-five-ten breathing pattern constitutes one round. Do this breathing pattern for ten rounds. You can use your fingers to note the completion of each round up to ten. When you have completed ten rounds, let your breathing return to normal.

Imagine that your body is weightless and that you are now floating on a gentle sea of kindness. The water is full of kindness that formed itself in response to you saying "thank you." Imagine that the kindness you are floating on is seeping into your skin, whether you see it, hear it, just know that it's happening, or feel it. All ways of perceiving are perfect—there's no best or better; there's just the unique way in which you are wired as an expression of the One Love that you are. How your experience happens for you is already beautiful. The waters of kindness easily enter through your skin, and kindness flows throughout your body, raising your vibrational rate. The kind waters sooth every nook and cranny of your being. Take your time. Let the waters automatically bring healing to your body, washing through you in waves, entering your heart, flowing into your mind, washing, washing, washing everything in kindness.

When you wish to move on, call golden light to surround you. The golden light is the light of the angelic realm, and it comes instantly in the very second you summon it. See, hear, sense, feel, or just know that you are now encased in golden light that extends six feet in all directions. It goes through any and all things around you—floors, walls, furniture—until it becomes a full six feet in diameter. Let this happen naturally; surrender to its happening. Give permission for your aura to be filled with angelic light. Float and let yourself rest as you enjoy the peace and freedom of golden blessings as you just breathe it in.

When you feel ready, call to the Archangel Michael. You can do this silently just with your thoughts, whisper his name, or call to him out loud—any and every way will work. Let yourself experience his arrival, whether you hear, see, feel, sense, or just know that he has come to you. Remember, the angels are always waiting for us to call upon them—it is their greatest joy to come to us when we do so. Take as long as you need in order to experience Michael's presence.

Once Michael is with you, ask him to please lift out of you imprints of pain that were made in the past. Take your time in allowing yourself to know that the work is being done. Your experience may be very subtle or strong. You may or may not be silent, cry, or even laugh out loud—there's no best or better. There's just the way it happens for you personally. Anything that occurs is normal and has happened to others before you. Just allow it to be and say, "Thank you, Michael," as the healing continues. You can add more words if you want to; you can ask for things that may start to rise up inside you as you float in the golden light in the company of this powerful archangel. Surrender to Michael's amazing powers to eliminate things you do not need or want.

When you feel ready, call to your own guardian angel and ask it to align itself all along the left side of your body so that it is touching your skin all down your left side. Ask your guardian angel to gently begin to send from itself into you as much of the beautiful love it carries as you need in order to replace the pain that Michael is taking away. Let it flow in slowly to start. Notice how it naturally begins to flow in faster as you get used to the feeling. Allow the inflow of angelic light to intensify, to heal you and to set you free to live your highest potential. Continue to say "thank you" to Michael and to your guardian angel. Don't be surprised if you fall asleep, since the energy of it is so strong. If you don't fall asleep, you will know when this angelic healing treatment is done.

Say a final "thank you" to Michael and to your angel at the end, or whenever you wake up.

This exercise can be repeated as much as, and whenever, you would like.

A pillow for thee will I bring,
Stuffed with down of angel's wing.
—RICHARD CRASHAW

CHAPTER 9

Angels Healing the Healer

In meditation, I became the vessel to receive deeper healing information from the angelic realm. Gabriel explained to me, "Whenever there is a spiritual wound, if that wound isn't cared for properly in the correct amount of time, a physical manifestation will appear wherever there is already a weakness in the body. You now need medical attention. We will help you to find your way to the right doctors."

So here I was, five years after the first pain attack, with Gabriel directing my search as I looked at doctors on the New York-Presbyterian/Columbia University Medical Center website. Gabriel told me whom to go to.

I went to a nephrologist, who gave me a complete exam and after a thoughtful interview sent me on to the urology department. Since the urologist he wanted me to see didn't take my insurance, once more I sat before the Columbia Presbyterian website with Gabriel, who pointed me to the right doctor. After another thorough exam on the day of my appointment, I soon got a call to schedule a nuclear test that would provide a clear picture of just how my kidneys were functioning.

On the day of the nuclear test, I was met outside the doors to the testing area by a technician I had worked with many times before when I had come with patients of Dr. Feldman. She was so kind. A doctor came in to give me the nuclear shot, and then I was put into a machine that took pictures of my kidneys continuously for twenty minutes.

At the end of the test, the technician and I laughed together at my reaction when she handed me a signed notice on hospital stationery. "This is your 'get out of jail free' letter, so don't lose it," she said. I could feel my eyes widening with surprise as she went on to explain, "You will be radioactive for a few days, so in case you set anything off, just show this letter to the police and everything will be fine." This being New York City with a police department ever vigilant in its work to keep us safe, I wasn't about to misplace that letter! I had heard before about individuals with medical nuclear substances in their bodies being stopped by the police.

I was called with the results of the test. I was very relaxed as my cell phone rang in my hand; my legs were up to midcalf in bubbling water, since I was in the midst of having a pedicure at my favorite nail salon in my neighborhood. That definitely made it easier to hear the news.

I knew I had been born with a genetic flaw—the ureter (slender tube) from my left kidney to my bladder was very narrow. The pictures from the nuclear test showed that that ureter had caused my left kidney to atrophy. It was now shrunken, obstructed, and very sick. That was exactly how my spiritual wounding had manifested, and thankfully, it was finally diagnosed and had a solution—removal of the kidney. I was told to call Dr. Ketan Badani to make a pre-surgery appointment.

Dr. Badani! I knew the angels were working overtime when I heard his name. While in operating rooms with Dr. Feldman and Dr. Rohde, anesthesiologists had more than once mentioned they felt it would be wonderful if I could bring Reiki to the patients of Dr. Badani, if I ever got the chance. I could never have imagined I was destined to meet him because I myself would become his patient!

I knew I was lucky to be in his capable hands. At the time, he was Director of Robotic and Minimally Invasive Surgery at New York-Presbyterian Hospital/Columbia University Medical Center and Associate Professor of Urology at Columbia University. His résumé is extensive and includes international accolades. His awards include America's Top Urologists and America's Top Surgeons for Robotic Surgery.

This is the doctor the angels had managed to get me to! At last! A diagnosis and a plan! Although on the one hand it was certainly intimidating to hear I needed a serious surgery, at least I would finally be free of all that had plagued me for so long. I would no longer have to live in fear that an attack would start up in one minute from now, tomorrow, on Tuesday to disrupt my important meeting, next month when

I have company coming for the holidays, later today when a client needs me in the operating room, etc.

I was already planning to have lunch with my son, John, and his darling fiancée, Dina, and our reservation came right on the heels of my getting the news. As we all sat down at our table, John could see I had something on my mind.

"Mom, what's up?" John asked, looking at me intently as he scooted his chair in under the table. When I told them I had just been notified I needed to have my kidney removed, the faces of both Dina and John registered shock. With so much pure love, John said to me, "Mom, I'll go into surgery with you so you can have Reiki." I had already thought about that.

"No, John, I wouldn't want you to have to face that, for more reasons than one. You know what's it's like in the operating room. I'll ask another Reiki master that I've trained," I replied. The relief I saw in his eyes was immediate.

I called the medium Lisa A. to let her know that the spiritual ties to the past were now going to be broken in the physical realm by my upcoming surgery. After my conversation with her, I was pondering who would be the best person to ask to come with me to the operating room.

"Here is your answer," whispered Gabriel as my phone rang. It was Lisa Wolfson, who had connected me with Lisa A. in the first place during her Reiki master training after seeing the 9/11 photograph on my computer screen. *Perfect!* I thought as soon as I heard her voice. Who better to assist me at such a crucial moment in my life, since Lisa's Reiki master in spirit is the Archangel Michael?

"Lisa, if the surgeon will allow it, would you consider going into the operating room with me?" I asked. "I need surgery myself now."

"Raven! Oh my God, it would be an honor to go with you into your surgery!" Lisa had already completed all of her training with me and was now a Reiki master teacher. The strength of our emotional bond was deep, and I knew I was being angel-led.

If Dr. Badani agreed to have Lisa come with me, we would all be making history together. I was about to hopefully receive Reiki from a Reiki master during my own surgery. And from a Reiki master I had personally trained with a doctor whose team had never had Reiki in his operating theater before.

Before my surgery, my sister, Sharon, who lives in Denver, took me down to Santa Fe, New Mexico. She was absolutely determined for me to see the miraculous stairway in the Our Lady of Light Chapel, also known as the Loretto Chapel, because she felt it would be a very powerful way that I could intensify my own connections to divinity in preparation for my surgery.

Sharon could never have known in advance just how important it was going to be for me to hold the memory of what we would experience together in that amazing chapel.

The history of the chapel began in 1852, when, after an arduous passage from Kentucky via paddle steamer and covered wagon, the Sisters of Loretto arrived in Santa Fe to build a convent, a school, and a chapel. When the chapel was built as a copy of a church in Paris, it ended up with a choir loft too high up in the rafters to be accommodated by an ordinary stairway without taking up most of the seating area for the congregation. This meant that the sisters would never be able to sing from their choir loft.

The sisters prayed, and shortly thereafter, a gray-haired man appeared with a donkey and a toolbox, saying he would like to build their stairway. He only had a hammer, a saw, and a T-square. He completed his work during the Christmas season, and when the mother superior went to pay him, he had disappeared. She went to the lumberyard to at least pay for the supplies and was told no lumber had been purchased.

What this mysterious carpenter had left behind was a spiral staircase that took up very little room and was self-standing. Thereafter, for more than one hundred years, the Sisters of Loretto ran up and down those stairs to sing with joy. Today, the stairway is closed for use to preserve it. In the recent past, two small supports were added to affix it to the wall because of the vibration of modern traffic.

Structural engineers and builders who have seen it proclaim they have no idea how the man built such a self-standing stairway that makes two complete circles and is perfect in every way. In 1997, a specimen of the wood from the Loretto Staircase was sent to Forrest Easley, an authority on the subject of trees with an impressive résumé, including work for the US government in timber management and research, as well as with the US Navy Research and Development Laboratory.

After conducting his research on the wood for more than two months, Mr. Easley showed up at the chapel in person to deliver his remarkable news. He reported that the stairway in the Loretto Chapel was made of a spruce of an unknown subspecies. It was a wood from an unexplained source. So where did the wood come from? And who is the person who built that stairway out of something not identifiable by one of the world's foremost experts?

Stepping in from the morning sunshine, Sharon and I came into the darkened entrance of the chapel and waited a moment, letting our eyes adjust to the light. There was a feeling of awe radiating from the people who were leaving as they passed us on their way out. Once we were accustomed to the change in light, we stepped through a threshold into the beauty of a simple chapel graced with wonderful stained glass windows, and into the presence of a divine miracle. I could feel angelic energy inside the chapel even before my eyes connected with its source. The staircase itself was radiating joy and light.

I sat in one of the pews next to the staircase and felt my heart open wide, wide, wide. The feeling of profound divinity came over me so strongly that my eyes filled with tears. I prayed from the depths of my heart to the One Love that my surgery would be a success and that the words in this very book would be able to produce to even a small degree what I was feeling inside that chapel.

In my moment of such true connection with the God/Goddess force, I knew in my heart that only an angel could have built that staircase. When one is in that state of glory and ecstasy, there is a connection to the divine that brings results in ways we can't begin to imagine. The feeling in the pit of my stomach let me know that my prayer to bring awareness of angelic love into the world was now planted firmly in forever. I could finally rest in the knowledge that I had truly asked properly. My sister was so right—I really needed to see that staircase and to feel the angelic energy left in the chapel—not only to write but also to be healed of my past, once and for all.

I could finally realize for myself what Gabriel had been saying about spiritual wounding. While sitting inside that chapel, something came awake inside me that had long been sleeping. In an experience similar to having my life flash before my eyes, I saw my experiences after 9/11 stripping me of my core belief in humankind. I realized that by seeing the violence of what humans had done to each other, my own connection to divinity had been eroded ever so slightly, day by day. That wounding had shut off a truly mystical part of my own life, and I had slowly stopped believing in the triumphant good inherent in humankind. In the slow erosion of my belief in humanity, I had lost a deep core belief in myself and had cut myself off from the deepest joys of being connected to the divine.

Feeling the angelic power inside the Loretto Chapel was like using spiritual smelling salts—it was as if I was being revived, out of a terrible dream, with my sister by my side and Gabriel right behind me. It was one of the most extraordinary experiences of my life.

After praying in the pew for my safety in the upcoming surgery, Sharon and I walked with reverence to the altar. We hugged each other as we stood before candles we lit at the altar.

"Sister, I'm so glad we came," I said to her. "Thank you so much for bringing me here."

With tears in her eyes, she said, "I'm glad we came, too. And this place reminds me that our family has always been blessed. I'm sure your surgery will be a success."

Before I left Denver, I began to think ahead to my upcoming Reiki training I was conducting in August. I thought, "Oh, I'll just schedule my kidney removal after the training." However, at 2:00 a.m. on the morning of my flight to leave Denver, another pain attack developed. By the time Sharon and I arrived at the airport for my morning flight, I was in excruciating pain and vomiting violently. I was also delirious and couldn't stand up straight because of the pain.

The Frontier Airline customer service staff took one look at me and sent me away from the counter to sit in a chair. My sister was explaining to them that we had called and there were no available seats out of Denver until the morning I was due to meet with my surgeon.

Frontier sent for a paramedic, who, after a brief assessment of my condition, consulted with my sister. The paramedic, who was a hospital professional, determined that nothing new was happening to me. After careful consideration, he deemed that I was safe to fly. Everyone agreed that the best thing for me was to get home so I could have my pre-surgery appointment with Dr. Badani, which was scheduled for two days later.

The Frontier staff jumped in to help me, and they were incredible. They allowed my sister to accompany me to the gate, so off I went in a wheelchair all the way to the door of the aircraft. Once inside the plane, I told the stewardess, "There's a very strong possibility I am going to throw up during this flight."

"No worries, people throw up all the time," she said. "Let me get you a garbage bag."

I know Gabriel was protecting me, because as soon as I had the bag clutched in my hand, I fell asleep with my head pressed up against the cool window. I don't remember taking off, or ever opening my eyes to look at even one cloud. I slept all the way to New York, and all I can remember from that flight are my dreams, which were all about being inside the Loretto Chapel and feeling the presence of angels.

As soon as the wheels of the plane touched the ground in New York, I lifted my head off the window and began to throw up into the big garbage bag the stewardess had given me more than four hours before. I struggled my way slowly off the plane and hobbled right into the arms of my son, who was waiting for me at the gate.

Just as we were leaving the airport, LaGuardia was shut down due to a crash landing. I hate to think of what would have happened to me if my flight had been delayed by even fifteen minutes—who knows where I would have ended up landing? Boston? Philadelphia? I had received yet another blessing.

Once I made it back to my apartment, the worst attack I had ever experienced raged on, leaving me depleted and disheartened. After staying in bed all of Tuesday, I was barely recovered enough to meet with Dr. Badani on Wednesday morning. Lisa and I had already planned that she would meet me at the hospital for the pre-surgery appointment in case Dr. Badani wanted to meet her.

I was really nervous that Dr. Badani would be averse to having Reiki in his operating theater. Feeling so weak and vulnerable from just having had such a severe attack, I didn't know how I would handle having to convince him to allow it if he had any reservations or objections.

I was already waiting for Dr. Badani when he walked into his office to begin the pre-surgery consultation. I jumped to my feet as he entered, feeling an immediate connection with him. His smile and the uplifting power of his life force emanating complete confidence put me at ease immediately.

Sticking out my hand to shake his, I said, "Dr. Badani, I'm so happy to meet you and very amazed at how this is happening." He raised his eyebrows in surprise as I continued, "I've been to surgery many times with Dr. Feldman, providing Reiki to his patients, and your name has been mentioned to me as someone who is a great surgeon." We continued to stand as I looked into his eyes. "Dr. Badani, I need to get right to the point. I just can't have the surgery without a Reiki master present."

With that he moved to his desk and we both sat down. Settling into his chair he said, "Well, I've never had anything so unusual in the operating room. I've heard of Reiki—my aunt does it—but I don't know what it is, and I don't know any Reiki masters, except for you as of right now."

"I have one with me, Dr. Badani. Her name is Lisa Wolfson, and she's in the waiting room."

"Do you want her to come in? It would be a pleasure to meet her!"

Dr. Badani explained, with Lisa taking notes for me, that my kidney was functioning at only 9 percent of its capability, which in medical terms meant that it was worthless. In my case, it was also causing danger to my life. With the threat of infection a real possibility, an emergency situation could arise that neither one of us would want to face. It was dire that it be removed as soon as possible.

Of course, I agreed. The idea of being sick even one more minute was too much for me to bear. The only thing we had to figure out was how to get Lisa into the operating room with us. He asked me to enlist Dr. Feldman's help with this, and I offered to call Patient Services to help us, as well.

The angels were in full swing. My surgery was set on Dr. Badani's calendar for less than two weeks in the future. After five years of suffering, I was finally on the fast track to being helped.

Since I was already in the hospital, Dr. Badani's thoughtful secretary scheduled all six pre-surgery tests to be done immediately. Lisa and I spent the next few hours with me having everything done so I wouldn't have to come back before surgery day.

After I got home from the hospital, emotions began to rip through me that I didn't understand. Anger seemed to be erupting from a bottomless pit, pouring out of me and coloring every other thing I felt. I broke down in tears just about every hour in terror, and I couldn't think clearly. It seemed like my whole life had upended itself as I raged out of control for several days without ceasing.

When I was finally able to remember I had a guardian angel (my inner state was so bad I had actually forgotten Gabriel!), I asked, "What is going on? Why is this happening to me? Why am I in this emotional roller coaster of anger and terror?"

Gabriel replied, "It's very important that you know how others truly feel when they get bad medical news. Your understanding so far has been empathic, but only to a point. Through these experiences, you can understand how people truly feel when they have to face things. You will be a better healer because of this."

I shared news of my upcoming surgery with family, friends, and those to whom I had taught Reiki. Love and healing energy began pouring in toward me from many spiritual corners. Tim Raven, my Celtic mystical friend, started prayers on my behalf to the Norse god Odin; Mascha and Karyn Boniface, my house hostesses in Glastonbury, vowed to light incense and candles on the day of my surgery on the Tor at the altar of the elven king Gwynn Ap Nudd. Lisa A., the medium who received the messages from my relatives, was lighting white candles daily and keeping me in her prayers to God and the angels, and Reiki was being sent to me from across the globe.

When I talked to Patient Services at the hospital on the Friday before my surgery, I was told that because I myself had requested Reiki, a protocol was now in place. A system to assist anyone else who might request Reiki during surgery had been created. I was asked if I would please allow any upcoming patients who wanted Reiki to call me. Of course I said yes.

The next day was the start of the weekend and some of my Reiki and meditation students came to my office to give me a group healing, which was absolutely incredible. It happened very last minute, and many who couldn't come in person sent healing from afar.

Before I got on the massage table to receive Reiki from eleven pairs of hands, I led a ceremony, filling the space with the love of the archangels, divinity, and the powers of air, fire, water, and earth.

The reports that came in afterward from those who had participated from afar were overwhelmingly beautiful. One woman felt faeries all around me, another said she met my inner child who had directed the light, and another said she saw angels working on me nonstop. I cried plenty to realize how many people were willing to stop everything they were doing in order to share their healing gifts with me. I had never felt so loved in all my life.

Later that night, in my own prayers and meditations I was asking that every shred of the past—all blockages to my happiness, all barriers and delusions—be removed from me so that when my kidney was taken, I would truly be free of everything that ever plagued me. I prayed to be free of what had held me back for such a long time. After all, I had five years of pain attacks during which I had to cancel classes, students, clients, and meetings, all of which had stunted the forward movement of my life.

I was so surprised when a female angel appeared before me in response to my prayers. She said her name was Sophia and that she had come to help me. Sophia said to me, "Yes, I am going to be taking all those dark strands around and through your kidney out of you and delivering them to the goddess Cerridwen. She wields the power that transforms darkness into light."

After a few moments of gazing at stars being born, Sophia went on to say, "Mother Mary will fill the space made inside your body by the removal of your kidney with pure love so you can move forward in freedom toward your greatest destiny." I was also told that I would be given new healing work to do with lots of people, training them as healers in partnership with angels.

I found it extraordinary, how everything fit together in such beauty and love. On the day of my surgery, August 6, 2013, I was awake before dawn. I was so glad that I hadn't had another pain attack in the two days beforehand, which had been a terrible fear of mine, keeping me in constant prayer. All I wanted was to be able to have the surgery, and if I'd had another attack, I would have been too sick and weak to have it.

At 7:30 a.m., John and Dina arrived at my apartment. My darling friend Grete Fries came by to drive me with my family to the hospital. I felt so lucky to be delivered to the Milstein doors, surrounded by so much love.

Lisa Wolfson had already arrived and was waiting in the lobby. I was so proud to see her in scrubs, about to go into her first surgery as a Reiki master, and I flew across the shiny floor under the vastness of the vaulted ceiling, into her waiting arms.

"Good morning, Raven," she said to me as she held me in a warm hug. "Don't worry about a thing; everything is going to be just great."

Up we all went in the elevator to the third floor registration area. As luck would have it, while I was sitting with the receptionist during the registration process, I saw Dr. Feldman pass by behind me. "Dr. Feldman!" I cried out, as I jumped out of my chair to receive a hug from him.

"Hello, Raven. Today's your big day! I'm sure everything is going to go very smoothly for you." I felt so encouraged, even as he sped away to his own surgery patients.

The receptionist put my identification band around my wrist, and we were sent to wait in chairs outside the pre-op area. We were early, so I was holding Lisa's hand as she sent Reiki through my palm, and I was enjoying the sunshine streaming in through the floor to ceiling windows that face the Hudson River. I didn't want to deny myself any feelings; it was very important to me that I feel everything and that I not suppress any of the emotions surrounding my surgery event.

When one of the nurses I knew came out to bring another waiting patient into the pre-op area, she was shocked to see me dressed in regular clothes with an ID band around my wrist.

"Oh, gosh, Raven! You're having surgery?" Her voice was filled with concern. By the time it was my turn to be brought into pre-op, the nursing staff had been alerted to the fact that I was coming in. It was heartwarming to be greeted by so much goodwill as my little troop made our way past the main desk and along the hallway to bed 12 ½. (I felt a little like Harry Potter on my way to the Hogwarts train—twelve is the only number in the lineup that has a ½ added to it—to skip thirteen, I suppose!)

My intake nurse was someone I knew well. We enjoyed each other's company as she greeted me and began her job of asking me all the usual questions that I was accustomed to hearing after being through this process with so many others. Then she shooed everyone out, pulling the curtains around me so I would have privacy as I changed into the hospital gown, the long, tight socks to accommodate the pressure cuffs that go on the lower legs during surgery, the little booties to keep my feet warm, and my blue surgery cap.

Once I was in all the gear, I climbed back onto the pre-op bed, and now I felt really alone. It was all too real, and even surreal. Looking down and seeing those items on my own body brought understanding into the depths of my life as to just how serious the surgery before me really was … and suddenly I was scared. I was so glad that Lisa was with me, and that she was coming with me to my greatest ordeal. I gave thanks to Gabriel and all the angels for making her presence possible.

I settled back in the bed and tried to relax as I waited for my family and Lisa to return. Then someone else I knew came in to take my vital signs. He was very kind and his soft voice worked magic upon my frayed nerves. Then a front desk supervisor who loves Reiki came to "talk shop" with me. She was excited to tell me she was taking her Reiki master training over the coming weekend in New Jersey.

When the star IV technician came in, her face registered shock to see me stretched out on the pre-op bed. Her eyes were wide as I explained my situation, and that I would be having Reiki during surgery with Dr. Badani. She held my left hand gently and said, "Take a deep breath," as she inserted the IV in a place close to my wrist. Even though this nurse is the best in the hospital at what she does, there was still pain when the needle was put in and then taped down.

"Okay, you're done," she said kindly. "That's the worst thing you will feel this whole day, and it's over."

I tried not to let all the familiarity keep me from feeling how others who don't know the players, and don't know what to expect, must feel. Yet I still couldn't help but know I was lucky when several other nurses and technicians came by to say hello and to wish me well.

Now I started giving orders to my family. I told John what to do to help Lisa, my husband where I wanted him to sit, Dina to go get something for her breakfast; I just couldn't settle down at all. John was seated at my feet, looking at me very intently. His eyes seemed to be saying, "Mom! Please just let us take care of you!"

I could feel his concern. But I had fought so hard for this moment—years of going into operating rooms with others, trying my best to explain Reiki to doctors and technicians during life-and-death situations, with people who I had come to love under my Reiki hands. It was hard to relinquish control. But it was time for me to begin learning this part of my lesson and to enjoy the reality of Reiki in a hospital, and soon for me in an operating room!

Although everything was expected to go well, we were still in a hospital with my very own surgery before us. So I finally just surrendered and let others take care of me. With John giving me Reiki through the bottoms of my feet and Lisa on my right sending Reiki through my arm and into my side, I could feel the power of the Archangels Michael and Gabriel. The light they made was soft all around me as I became so calm I started to fall asleep.

While drifting off, I was very aware of how important it was to let myself have the experiences before me. I had been down this very same road with so many patients, but I'd never had surgery myself. I was laying my body down on an operating table, hoping for the best, just like them.

Yes, it was wonderful to know the order in which things would happen, and it was certainly more than special to be surrounded by hospital personnel who knew me. But the bottom line was this was a serious surgery I was about to have, and the reality of that fact never left my awareness. There was still the possibility I might not come out of this in the way that I hoped to.

When Dr. Badani came in to say good morning, I was really happy, since that meant we were getting close to going into the OR. His smile was so reassuring, and he greeted us with real warmth. His calm confidence was such a blessing, and I felt very soothed by his presence as he sent everyone from the room in order to mark my left side with magic marker as an indication for everybody in the operating room that this was the kidney to be removed.

Once the anesthesia doctor came in, asking me all the questions they always ask and going through what to expect, it wasn't long before I was kissing my family goodbye, savoring a sweet moment with each one of them. I then bravely grabbed Lisa's hand as we began to follow the anesthesiologist.

With one last look back at my beloveds, I turned with Lisa to walk down the maze of familiar corridors. I already knew that because I was headed for robotic surgery, a bigger OR than I was accustomed to being in was needed to hold all the equipment. I let myself feel the terror of walking toward an operating room and squeezed Lisa's hand, so grateful for her calm presence, knowing she would be there with me through the thick of it.

As Lisa and I came through the operating room doors on the heels of the anesthesiologist, there was a hush that came over the room. We continued to hold hands as we followed him to the operating table at center stage. I noticed that everyone stopped what he or she was doing for a brief moment and turned to gaze at us. It was confusing to me; it almost

felt like they were bowing to us, something I had never experienced before when entering an operating room. At first
I didn't understand why—were they simply welcoming Reiki
into their sphere without resistance? It was only natural for
me to tune in to the energy around us to figure it all out.

When I checked in to "see," I realized the hospital staff
was exuding feelings of reverence. That's when I knew it was
because the Archangels Gabriel and Michael had entered the
operating room with us. Everyone in the room felt it, and
even if they didn't know what it was, they still couldn't help
themselves. They had almost bowed in the presence of the
archangels.

I lay myself down on the table with the help of the nurses
and technicians, and terror shot through my whole being as I
was being strapped down on the table. "Don't leave me, Lisa,
please don't leave me." I felt the panic of the child who had
gone through the surprise tonsillectomy when I was just a little girl rising up inside me. "Don't worry, Raven. I won't leave
you for a minute, I promise you."

I held out my right arm, laying it on the armrest, and Lisa
took my hand, while the anesthesiologist began administering the drugs to bring me under. The last thing I remember
was feeling like I was floating on a raft on top of water with
angels all around me.

What Gabriel had told me about spiritual wounding was
what Dr. Badani and his team encountered inside my body.

My spiritual wounds had become dangerously physical. Though atrophied and therefore shrunken in size, my left kidney was dilated and infected and thickly scarred from all the pain attacks. The scar tissue had practically glued it to the inside of my body. Because of all the scarring, it was very difficult to remove and it was an extremely challenging surgery for the team.

When my kidney was finally out and the team saw it, Dr. Badani was very happy it hadn't burst during any of my pain episodes. There's no telling what would have happened to me if I had waited any longer for the surgery.

Lisa told me that I had trouble waking up after the kidney removal was over. Just like I had done for another, this time it was me who was brought back out of anesthesia by Reiki and Lisa. When the doctors couldn't wake me up, she came to me and took my hand, calling my name. "Raven, come back. The surgery is over." That's when I finally opened my eyes.

There's a lot I don't remember that happened right after surgery, and even in the days following. I don't remember being in the post-op area. The first thing I remember with any clarity is slitting my eyes open to see my husband sitting in a chair at the foot of my bed in a hospital room I had no recollection of being brought to. Dr. Badani came in to see me and to tell me personally what he had already told my family: that all had gone well.

"Your kidney was really stuck inside you by all the scar tissue," he said, "so we had a time getting it out, but you don't have to worry about it anymore. It's gone." He went on to say, "Lisa was great in the operating room. She was wonderful, and I e-mailed Dr. Feldman as soon as your surgery was over to let him know you were okay. My team will come see you in the morning, but what you need right now is rest."

Following the doctor's orders, I promptly fell asleep.

But I wasn't alone. When I opened my eyes again, it was dark outside and there were two very tall angels standing guard over me. I was too tired to ask who they were.

The two angels were brilliant white light and filled up all the space from floor to ceiling between my bed and the big window beyond. I felt comforted by their presence and it seemed so natural that they would be there. I could tell that Gabriel was there, too, yet I couldn't see him. It felt to me like he was busy doing healing work inside my body.

My eyes were heavy and kept closing, but I could see the angel guards every time I opened them, and their light was shining in through my eyelids whenever I closed my eyes. I fell back asleep.

At 3:00 a.m. I woke up again. The two angels were still there and Gwynn Ap Nudd, the elven king, was sitting by my bed, holding my hand. The minute I saw him I thought, *Wow, Mascha and Karyn really did a powerful ceremony on the Tor!* He didn't say anything, and I was so tired, I just fell back to sleep.

I don't know how things were decided in the higher realms while I slept, but when I next opened my eyes, it was dawn, all spiritual visitors except Gabriel were gone, and I knew I wouldn't die. Instead, I went home later that afternoon and healed faster than anyone could believe.

When I called Tim Raven in Glastonbury a few days later and told him Gwynn had come to sit with me in the hospital, he paused for quite a while on the other end of the phone. I knew he was checking in with his spirit guides, and when he finally spoke, it was in a very quiet voice. "Raven, this is really significant. Gwynn could have given you your wish to live in Glastonbury."

"Do you mean I could have died and my spirit could have gone with him?" I asked.

"Yes, but instead he's going to start teaching you the secrets of faerie healing." I felt Gabriel's delight as my heart rejoiced. I was glad to hear such news, and Gabriel was happy for me to hear it.

This is a perfect time to explain yet again how we are all part of the One. Humans, angels, faeries, elves, trees, flowers, animals, water, air, fire, and earth—we are all in Oneness, if we can only just realize it. As the angels say, there is no separation, and my life is proof. There, in my hospital room, I was guarded by the angels and attended to by the faerie king of the ancient elven race, a being even older than humankind. The angels and the Faerie Lord had no problems, and never have had problems, with each other—it's only humankind that label expressions of divinity as "good" or "bad."

I know it is my mission to build a bridge between so many things—allopathic and alternative medicine, traditional and nontraditional belief systems, what we see with our eyes and the spiritual world behind it. I must find a way, with the help of the angels, to show what's really true, through the power of love.

My Final 9/11 Closure

On September 19, 2013, in Central Park, celebrating the full moon and the fall equinox with my spiritual community, we all stood together with a goblet filled with water from the Chalice Well mixed with water from the White Spring and some from the reservoir that supplies New York City. I raised the goblet up to the heavens and said some prayers before resting it on the step at the very edge of the Lake behind the famous Bethesda Fountain—the fountain in the shape of an angel.

All my kindred stood behind me with candles now lit with the flame from the End of the Mayan Calendar Winter Solstice Fire of 2012. With great emotion, I called in the archangels and prayed to the goddess of New York, who dwells in the water. I asked that She accept the things I came to release to Her, and to bless those held within them with everlasting joy and life.

With prayers complete, in the wild magic of the night, with stars shining on the surface of the Lake, I threw a piece of glass given to me by a police officer into the magical waters of the Lake. Lisa A. told me that a woman had been the last person to look through the glass before she died at the World Trade Center. Next I threw in a very small vial of dust that had been scooped up from the ground by a friend of mine two days after 9/11.

These last physical remains of my involvement with the events of September 11 went into the water for transformation. And when I emptied the goblet of its sacred contents to mix its holy magic with the powers of the Lake, my 9/11 service was really, truly, finally over.

Since this part of my personal healing story has come to its end, I get to make a prayer. "To the Divine One Love, I promise to stand with Gabriel and all the angels for as long as I am blessed to walk upon the sacred Earth. I will honor the seen and unseen Spirits of kindness in all the dimensions that grace our world as part of the One. I pray that we as humans can love one another and appreciate the good that surrounds us, both in what we can see and what we don't see with our physical eyes, but only with our hearts. May we come to appreciate all of the magic around us, everywhere! Blessed be."

I'm hoping that by having shared the odyssey of my healing, many more people can begin to turn to the angels to receive healing for their spiritual wounding. I feel this is important, because recent research has revealed that PTSD can even contribute to the breathing problems of those who worked at Ground Zero. Certainly that is only one more of the dramatic examples of how what we now know as spiritual wounding can create physical problems, although the wounding doesn't have to take place on a world stage. Trauma that can result in a physical manifestation of disease can come from anywhere. As examples, it can originate from being abused as a child, living with a violent person, or sometimes just from passing by a horrific automobile accident. For those who are ultrasensitive, it can even come from seeing tragic events on television.

I'm now going to include an exercise, which is to prevent spiritual wounding for anyone who is in an area or a situation that is dangerous. I can't stress enough how significant this teaching from the Archangels Michael and Gabriel really is. This is the information I was meant to bring through via my own spiritual wounding and eventual kidney removal.

Exercise:
Part One: Repairing Spiritual Wounding

This is best done while sitting. Call to the Archangel Michael and ask him to fill your aura with his blue light of protection. This means you will be surrounded by translucent blue light that extends away from your skin six feet in all directions.

The presence of the blue light alone is powerful, yet the most profound benefits come from the light spinning around and through you. So with your focus, intention, imagination, or pretending skills—however it works best for you—begin to move the blue light in a counterclockwise direction.

It helps to focus on one spot, so as you begin, either see, hear, sense, or know the blue light moving into your left hip, around the back of you, and out your right hip, then crossing in front of you, moving in on the left again around the back, out on the right, and so on. Let the blue light begin to spin faster and faster in the counterclockwise direction. Let yourself notice that just like the light is spinning in your hips, the blue light all around you is also spinning, passing through every part of you.

Ask Michael to take over and to spin the light himself on your behalf. As soon as you ask, the translucent blue light begins to spin blazingly fast, even on a cellular level. This is when you ask the Archangel Michael to remove from you any and all things that have lodged themselves in you that you don't need or want—things that are harmful and things that hold you back, whether they are physical, emotional, mental, or spiritual.

The blue light spins faster still, and any harmful things are automatically whirled out of you and spun far away from you by centrifugal force. Stay with this for as long as you want or need to.

When you feel done and wish to end the exercise, simply say, "Thank you, Archangel Michael," and ask him to stop the spin. You may now ask the Archangel Gabriel to spin the energy in and around you in the opposite direction to bring the creative force of the Universe into you and to seal you in love.

Part Two: When in Danger

If you must remain in a dangerous environment of any kind, follow all the above instructions, but don't end the exercise. Instead, ask Archangel Michael to push the blue light closest to you out into the farthest three feet of your aura. In other words, Michael draws the light from directly around you out into what becomes a band of translucent blue light that fills the outer three feet of your energy field.

Right now, nothing can touch you; nothing can get into you. Archangel Michael is a band of translucent blue light spinning faster than lightning around you to keep you ultra safe! You can keep this going for as long as you need the protection.

When you are in a safer environment, you can end the exercise by saying, "Thank you, Archangel Michael," and asking him to stop the spin. You may now ask the Archangel Gabriel to spin the energy in and around you in the opposite direction to bring the creative force of the universe into you and to seal you in love.

Part Three: Healing in a Dangerous Environment

If you are doing healing work in a dangerous or uncomfortable environment, do parts one and two above, but don't end the exercise.

Once the translucent blue band is spinning in the outer half of your aura as described above, you can draw green energy up from the earth through the bottoms of your feet. Move the green light upward in your body all the way to the top of your head. Then receive white light from above through the top of your head. Allow the green and the white lights to entwine themselves into a double helix of balanced power.

Now ask your guardian angel to move into the space right around you as golden light. Keep these patterns of light within and around you for as long as you are working in any emergency or intense situation.

When you are done with your work, close down the double helix by asking it to stop. Travel to safety with the outer three-foot band of blue light continuing to spin. When you are safe, say, "Thank you, Archangel Michael," and ask him to stop the spin. You may now ask the Archangel Gabriel to spin the energy in and around you in the opposite direction to bring the creative force of the universe into you and to seal you in love.

These things I warmly wish for you:
Someone to love, some work to do,
A bit o' sun, a bit o' cheer,
And a guardian angel always near.
—IRISH BLESSING

Epilogue

When I am hearing Gabriel's words, the feelings they evoke in me are so powerful they fill every part of my being. Talking about the experiences of hearing Gabriel is one step removed. And writing about them? Well, having my brain occupied with forming sentences while my fingers type words onto pages leaves the real power up to the angels themselves. They are the ones who fill in the emotions for readers, touching hearts and minds with the hope and healing their love truly brings, and I trust they've done a good job with that for you.

My life itself is the only canvas on which I have to show the power of angels. My one-on-one work with Gabriel has not changed very much over the years. I still sit with my journal, asking questions and receiving answers. The only difference is how much the questions themselves have changed and the requests I make. For example, I always ask Gabriel to send the correct mix of people to my workshops or to my Reiki trainings, and in the midst of that kind of request I often get profound advice about my career.

Ever since my surgery, my connections with the angels have intensified even more. When Lisa Wolfson brought the Archangel Michael with her into the OR, I got to experience up close and personal just how much he was protecting me and fighting for my life. Since then, I've been graced with the opportunity to work with Archangel Michael as a constant—he and Gabriel walk on either side of me now.

As Gabriel predicted, because I've been a patient myself now, I know from an even deeper place why Reiki is necessary during surgery. I can advocate more passionately than ever before because I understand how terrifying surgery really is when you are the one who has to go through it. And because Lisa was with me, I now understand what kind of love a person feels for their Reiki master, and the level of gratitude that naturally occurs from facing the OR together.

When I went to my post-surgery follow-up appointment with Dr. Badani, he was thrilled with my speedy recovery. After examining me, he told me unequivocally how impressed he was with Lisa's professionalism and obvious training, and I was so glad for his reaction. Yet there was something very specific I wanted to know.

"Dr. Badani," I asked him, "how was it for *you* to have Reiki in your operating room?"

His eyes lit up as he said, "Well, let me tell you, your case was a difficult one, but even so, everything went very smoothly. Everyone noticed how easily it went."

"Oh?"

"Yes, with all that scarring, it was a struggle to get your kidney out, and with all the challenges that posed, everything still went perfectly. During the whole procedure, Lisa was very calm, and she brought such a feeling of peace into the room. I'm down for this, I think it's great!"

Not long afterward, Dr. Badani came to my office to experience Reiki firsthand. As always, I opened the session by calling in the angels. From the start, the power of the energy pouring through me and into Dr. Badani was extraordinarily powerful—more than either of us expected.

I couldn't assess whether the intensity of the session was because Dr. Badani was very receptive to energy, or whether he was in dire need of it to restore himself of all he must expend as a doctor saving people's lives. When I moved along his right side and held his hand between mine to administer Reiki, Gabriel whispered to me, "The right hand of God." He was letting me know that Dr. Badani is doing work that is directed by the One Love. I became very emotional.

Next, I went to stand at the foot of the table to send Reiki through the bottoms of Dr. Badani's feet. Gabriel came to stand behind me, and he put his hands on top of mine. The whole room filled up with angels, and for the first time in my life, some of them were the little ones called cherubs; I'd never seen them before—not even in childhood. Gabriel asked me to continue to send energy though the bottoms of

Dr. Badani's feet for an unusually long time. I didn't question why; I just kept following Gabriel's instructions. I was next directed up to his head and told to place my hands on his shoulders. I could then feel a strong current of energy streaming through me that ran out of my palms, down Dr. Badani's arms, and into his hands. The current was so strong that I didn't want to move from that position and stayed there until the very end of the session.

When his session was over, Dr. Badani sat up and reported everything to me, just like a true scientist. "I didn't know how I was going to stay still for an hour—in the beginning my mind was jumping from one patient to another, but then I just started following the sensations I was having." He next commented on how the session had reconnected him to the importance of physical touch and all it can convey. He explained that the feeling of energy coming through my hands had guided him to a place of deep rest. "I've been up since 5:30 a.m., running like crazy all day, but now I feel like I just slept for three days." When I told him about the points at which Gabriel and the angels were most pronounced during the session, he acknowledged that he had felt those things and that at the end, when the currents were running down his arms, he slipped into a state akin to being in deep meditation.

Incredibly, Dr. Badani has invited me and my team to work with his patients. This means angels are advancing even further into modern medicine as we do our work as Reiki masters, assisted by their divine presence. And furthermore, this means that my surgery has brought more amazing results than I could have ever imagined—which so often happens when we ask the angels for their help.

The purpose of this book has been to inspire you to shine in your own unique way by connecting with the angels. With angelic aid, we can remember who we really are and live our own truth. No matter where you live, what you do, or how things may have gone up until now, the angels can help you live a life of majesty, glory, and fulfillment, just like you were always meant to.

Overcoming adversity and finding happiness within are the most important aspects of our "mission" as human beings in this time period we find ourselves in. Why? It's because inner joy is a doorway to our own evolution as humankind. The entire angelic realm works together whenever we ask them to open doors inside the hearts of people in order to foster understanding and happiness. If, as a general rule of thumb, we ask the angels to help every person around us, the people we encounter in the day-to-day will be inspired, which will only bring better results into our own daily lives.

When one person is happy, the energy of that higher frequency of joy they emanate can touch a resonance inside others. And so it goes—one by one, hearts can be opened to happiness, love, understanding, and true prosperity. This is why it's so important to walk in partnership with angels every day.

Don't think angels are above us; they need us as much as we need them, and its only by working together that we can assure the little heart door inside the people we encounter can really open. In this time period that seems to have activated a level of insanity all around us in response to the shift, we are wise to access help from angels as a love booster. Humans have ego based in fear, which can cause jealousy or other harsh emotions to rise up from the ego's terror of losing control. In other words, when we walk with angels, we give others a much better chance of responding to a higher vibration, leading to their true path of inspired happiness!

You might think to yourself that this all sounds very well and good, but how does happiness really apply to helping others in daily life? Well, I do have proof from my own experiences. As I've shared with clients, students, colleagues, and friends the many happiness-producing things angels have brought to me over the years, they have likewise been inspired to work toward their own happiness. Like attracts like, so the happier one is, the better their life is.

The truth is, committing to your happiness, and especially by working with angels, a path forms before your feet. You may not realize the path is forming, but you will notice that your happiness begins to wake up and naturally spreads itself to others, which makes life rewarding and magical!

What is inside you is so profound and so full of love that there just aren't any words with which to describe it. You are glorious and wondrous and capable of changing not just your own life, but even the course of history! It doesn't matter if you are a truck driver, an actor, a factory worker, a teacher, a mother, or a father—the power within you is boundless!

My telling is coming to an end, but the story doesn't end here. It continues with you, gentle reader. We are at the end of the book, which is really just the beginning of the ever-unfolding wonder of working with angels.

Gabriel gets the last word, as he wishes to speak to you directly, and here are his words:

As we have said before, we wish to bring love to you. We hope you will allow us to work with you toward the manifestation of more goodness. We long for this communication. All are welcome! We wish to bring gladness into the hearts and minds of many people and thank you for choosing this path.

Further Resources

Angels

Byrne, Lorna. *Angels in My Hair*. New York: Harmony Books, 2008.

Lysette, Chantel. *The Angel Code: Your Interactive Guide to Angelic Communication*. Woodbury, MN: Llewellyn Publications, 2010.

Marshall, Judith. *My Conversations with Angels: Inspirational Moments with Guardian Spirits*. Woodbury, MN: Llewellyn Publications, 2012.

Profiles of the Archangels: http://www.examiner.com/article/profiles-of-4-archangels-michael-raphael-gabriel-uriel

Thayer, Stevan J. *Interview with an Angel*. New York: Dell, 1997.

Reiki

Keyes, Raven. *The Healing Power of Reiki: A Modern Master's Approach to Emotional, Spiritual & Physical Wellness.* Woodbury, MN: Llewellyn Publications, 2012.

Petter, Frank Arjava. *Reiki Fire: New Information about the Origins of the Reiki Power, A Complete Manual.* Twin Lakes, WI: Lotus Press, 1997.

Stein, Diane. *Essential Reiki: A Complete Guide to an Ancient Healing Art.* Berkeley, CA: The Crossing Press, 1995.

Vennells, David. *Reiki for Beginners: Mastering Natural Healing Techniques.* Woodbury, MN: Llewellyn Publications, 1999.

Reiki Training

Raven's website: http://ravenkeyes.com

Canadian Reiki Association: http://www.reiki.ca

Inspiration Reiki (Tamara Maury):
http://www.inspirationreiki.net

The Reiki Training Program (Eileen Dey):
http://www.reikitrainingprogram.com

Additional Resources

Breast Cancer Surgery: Dr. Sheldon Marc Feldman:
http://www.columbiadoctors.org/prof/smfeldman

Columbia University Medical Center Book Recommendations: http://www.columbiasurgery.org/news/book
.html

Medical Research on Reiki Therapy:
http://www.reikimedresearch.org

More on the Staircase at Loretto Chapel in Santa Fe, New
Mexico: http://www.sott.net/article/225775-Analysis-of
-Sample-From-Miraculous-Stairs-in-Santa-Fe-Found
-Unknown-Species-of-Wood

Plastic Surgery: Dr. Christine Rohde: http://asp.cumc
.columbia.edu/facdb/profile_list.asp?uni=chr2111
&DepAffil=Surgery

Robotic Surgery: Dr. Ketan K. Badani:
http://www.mountsinai.org/profiles/ketan-k-badani

Music I Listened to While Writing

Michael Pestalozzi

Niall

Seal

Joni Mitchell

Led Zeppelin (especially "Stairway to Heaven")

To Write to the Author

If you wish to contact the author or would like more information about this book, please write to the author in care of Llewellyn Worldwide Ltd. and we will forward your request. Both the author and publisher appreciate hearing from you and learning of your enjoyment of this book and how it has helped you. Llewellyn Worldwide Ltd. cannot guarantee that every letter written to the author can be answered, but all will be forwarded. Please write to:

Raven Keyes
℅ Llewellyn Worldwide
2143 Wooddale Drive
Woodbury, MN 55125-2989

Please enclose a self-addressed stamped envelope for reply, or $1.00 to cover costs. If outside the U.S.A., enclose an international postal reply coupon.

GET MORE AT LLEWELLYN.COM

Visit us online to browse hundreds of our books and decks, plus sign up to receive our e-newsletters and exclusive online offers.

- • Free tarot readings • Spell-a-Day • Moon phases
- • Recipes, spells, and tips • Blogs • Encyclopedia
- • Author interviews, articles, and upcoming events

GET SOCIAL WITH LLEWELLYN

Find us on Facebook
www.Facebook.com/LlewellynBooks

Follow us on twitter™
www.Twitter.com/Llewellynbooks

GET BOOKS AT LLEWELLYN

LLEWELLYN ORDERING INFORMATION

Order online: Visit our website at www.llewellyn.com to select your books and place an order on our secure server.

Order by phone:
- • Call toll free within the U.S. at 1-877-NEW-WRLD (1-877-639-9753)
- • Call toll free within Canada at 1-866-NEW-WRLD (1-866-639-9753)
- • We accept VISA, MasterCard, and American Express

Order by mail:
Send the full price of your order (MN residents add 6.875% sales tax) in U.S. funds, plus postage and handling to: Llewellyn Worldwide, 2143 Wooddale Drive Woodbury, MN 55125-2989

POSTAGE AND HANDLING

STANDARD (U.S. & Canada):
(Please allow 12 business days)
$25.00 and under, add $4.00.
$25.01 and over, FREE SHIPPING.

INTERNATIONAL ORDERS (airmail only):
$16.00 for one book, plus $3.00 for each additional book.

Visit us online for more shipping options. Prices subject to change.

FREE CATALOG!

To order, call
1-877-
NEW-WRLD
ext. 8236
or visit our
website

A Modern Master's Approach to Emotional,
Spiritual & Physical Wellness

the
Healing Power
of
Reiki

Foreword by Mehmet C. Oz, MD

RAVEN KEYES

The Healing Power of Reiki

A Modern Master's Approach to Emotional, Spiritual & Physical Wellness

RAVEN KEYES

The ancient art of Reiki has the power to heal our minds, bodies, and spirits in ways few of us can imagine. The first Reiki Master to practice in an operating room under the supervision of Dr. Mehmet Oz, author Raven Keyes has brought Reiki to the defining events of our time. With engaging prose, Keyes tells moving stories of giving Reiki to rescue workers at Ground Zero, PTSD survivors, professional athletes, trauma patients, and those suffering from crippling emotional pain. Keyes offers inspirational experiences of connecting with angels and spirit guides, and shares the joys and pains of working with patients, their loved ones, and their communities. Through stories and meditations, readers are filled with hope and a sense of good will. Helpful exercises and meditations are included to invite healing and provide the opportunity to engage with Reiki energy more deeply.

978-0-7387-3351-7, 288 pp., 5 ³/₁₆ x 8   **$16.99**

HEAL YOURSELF

with

ANGELS

Meditations,

Prayers,

and

Guidance

PATRICIA PAPPS

Heal Yourself with Angels
Meditations, Prayers, and Guidance
Patricia Papps

Contact the angels who can heal your life and the world. Illuminate your spirit while bringing peace to your soul and calmness to your mind. Learn which angels to contact for specific problems, such as depression, anxiety, lack of confidence, and money problems.

With the power of angel meditation, you can put your life on a new course. In *Heal Yourself with Angels*, author Patricia Papps shows how to work with the angels to create miracles and make your most cherished wishes come true. Learn how to connect with angel energy for protection, relationship issues and loneliness, removing negative blocks, combating evil, healing illness and disease, protecting the weak, sending love into the world, increasing creativity, and more.

978-0-7387-3703-4, 312 pp., 5 x 7   **$15.99**
